FACES of GRIEF
Overcoming the Pain of Loss

Veronica Semenova

SO-BTT-706

ISBN-13: 978-1511426411

ISBN-10: 1511426411

Important Note

This book is not intended as a substitute for medical advice or treatment.
Any person with a condition requiring medical attention should consult a qualified medical professional or suitable therapist.

About the Author

Veronica Semenova, Ph.D. is a private practicing psychologist working with a variety of psychological conditions, including depression, anxiety, grief, bereavement, coping with chronic and critical illness, fear of death, caregiver issues, aging issues, interpersonal and relationship issues. She is a member of the American Psychological Association, Psi Chi International Honor Society in Psychology, and the Association for Psychological Therapies.

Dr. Semenova is the author of "Learn How to Cope with Death, Loss, Grief, and Bereavement - Helpful Tips from the Cognitive-Behavioral Therapy".

Visit Dr. Semenova's website at www.vsemenova.com for more information.

Book Description

Many books are written about grief: what it is and how to deal with it - but no loss is the same. The intensity of grief depends on many different factors. Grief varies between young and old and between cultures and religions, and depends on levels of existing dysfunction and on the nature of death (if the death was expected or sudden). It depends on previous experiences with death and attachment styles, and, of course, interpersonal factors play a very important role, as well. Grief also depends on the personality of the bereaved and the type of relationship the bereaved had with the deceased. Unprocessed emotions in that relationship, conflicts, repressed feelings, and unspoken words all come out in grief and weigh heavily upon a grieving person, often complicating recovery.

In Faces of Grief, I share many stories of grief from my psychotherapy practice and explain how grief can be anticipatory, disenfranchised, or complicated. I also discuss the common myths about grief. All stories reveal the extensive work that the bereaved has to go through to enable them to come to terms with guilt, self-reproach, and the pain of grief.

I also provide practical information on how to help yourself or your grieving loved one, how to talk to children about death and grief, and what not to say to a person who is grieving. This book will be useful for anyone going through bereavement and grief, and for those supporting them.

Table of Contents

CHAPTER ONE

Losses in our Life

"The deep pain that is felt at the death of every friendly soul arises from the feeling that there is in every individual something which is inexpressible, peculiar to him alone, and is, therefore, absolutely and irretrievably lost."
- Arthur Schopenhauer (1788-1860)

There comes a time in everyone's life when the death of a loved one - a spouse, parent, child, sibling, or a friend - enters the room. Some people experience it as kids when one of their elder relatives dies, while others do not experience loss until later on in life. In some tragic cases, early loss occurs when the parent of a young child passes away. Death is one sure thing, like birth, that happens to all living beings.

Many of us remember the first time the word death was spoken: when we found a dead insect, when a family pet died, or when an elderly relative passed away. These events generate acute curiosity. Children may observe people crying, parents mourning, or funeral arrangements being made. Parents often rush to comfort the child and offer a consoling explanation ("Don't worry: Granddad is just in a deep sleep, and his soul is traveling to heaven."). Different stories of eternal life, meeting again in heaven, being re-born or resurrected, and so on are shared with children. I imagine you've heard some of these explanations, too.

Later on, children find out that death has nothing to do with "deep sleep". By then, anxiety and fear have conquered their minds. In fact, some children are afraid to sleep as a result of "death explanations", and their parents may wonder why. If you were told that dying is like going to sleep, then it would be hard to sleep without worrying about dying.

I can't repeat this enough to parents who need to explain a death in the family to their young child: Please do not hide the truth. Children are able to cope with the knowledge of death. At different ages, this understanding is different, but the truth is better than any of the stories commonly used as explanations.

In fact, there is often a relationship between sleep and death. Sleep and the loss of consciousness that takes place when we sleep is thought by many to be a "death rehearsal" that happens to us every night. (By the way, in Greek mythology, Thanatos (death) and Hypnos (sleep) are twin brothers.)

One way or another, the myths of dying are one day dismissed. That usually happens around adolescence, as young individuals realize their own and their loved ones' mortality. The end of belief in fairy tales brings about the first existential crisis: the end of childhood and the beginning of adolescence, with the accompanying strong animosities that teenagers often display. The first loss leaves a very deep scar; and even if it happened very early on in life, the consequences of reactions to that loss (words that were exchanged by grown-ups at the time, or rituals observed) all define the ways in which future losses will be experienced and handled.

In the chapter "Grief in Children", I will describe how children see and understand death at different developmental ages and why it is important to be honest and present information about death and loss in a way that is understandable to a child, which does not foster myths, fears, or anxiety.

No matter when the next loss happens and how close the relationship was with the person who passed away, grief is a natural reaction to loss. Nobody is ever prepared for grief. You can't learn to deal with grief until the feeling overwhelms you, bringing with it sadness, anger at destiny, despair, and acute loneliness. Anger resolves over time - we learn to live with our loss, and there comes a time when it doesn't hurt as much as it did - but why doesn't the sadness go away? Why do we still hurt every time we come close to the next anniversary of our loved one's birth or death, and why does flipping through pictures or letters bring so much heartache? If grief is a natural reaction to loss, then how long is it normal for that reaction to last?

I will answer these and many more questions in this book. In fact, there are so many myths surrounding grief - what's normal and what's not, how the bereaved should be "handled", and what to say to a grieving person - that it would require a set of books just to go over all the myths and resolve many misconceptions. Whether the grieving person is you yourself or if you are reading this to find some helpful advice for someone close to you who is dealing with the loss of a loved one, I am sure this book will provide the necessary tools and support to help you through this difficult time.

Sadly, our society tends to impose rules on what is acceptable in grief and what's not. How often do you hear that mourning a loss should not exceed one year? So, according to this logic, after precisely 365 days, a grieving person is expected to magically stop crying and feeling sad? It does not happen that way. Grief, even one year after a loss, may feel overwhelming and cause depression, loneliness, anxiety, and the feeling that the deceased is still present and continues to communicate.

Not many people are able to come to terms with their loss at the end of the first year, and some people may require as much as three to four years to achieve emotional stability. With some losses, the pain is still sharp even decades later. Replacing the deceased in one's life does not end grief. For example: a new marriage does not stop a deceased spouse from grieving, while having another child does not stop parents from grieving for their deceased child.

Many books are written about grief, what it is, and how to deal with it, but many people still struggle to come to terms with the loss of their loved ones. Indeed, no loss is the same. You cannot just come up with a soothing formula that fits everyone.

I find, in my work, that the intensity of grief depends on many different factors. Grief varies between young and old and between cultures and religions, and depends on the levels of existing dysfunction and on the nature of death (if the death was expected or sudden). It depends on previous experiences with death and attachment styles, and, of course, interpersonal factors play a very important role, as well. Grief also depends on the personality of the bereaved and the type of relationship the bereaved had with the deceased. Unprocessed emotions in that relationship, conflicts, repressed feelings, and unspoken words all come out in grief and weigh heavily upon the grieving person, often complicating recovery. It takes a long time and a lot of work to go through these feelings and identify those that cause pain.

In the chapter "Types of Losses", I will talk about differences between the loss of a spouse, a parent, a child, a sibling, or a loss through suicide. I hope that some of the examples I present in this book will show you what type of emotional pain needs to be dealt with in the process of coping with grief.

Grief may be experienced not just after the death of a loved one, but can follow any form of catastrophic personal loss. This can include the loss of a job or income, the breakup of a major relationship or divorce, imprisonment, a diagnosis of infertility, chronic or terminal illness, the loss of a home from fire, a natural disaster and/or many other tragic events in life.

The stages of grief we go through to accept the loss and to reconstruct our lives are common to any catastrophic loss: denial, anger, bargaining, depression, and finally, acceptance. We will discuss each stage in the chapter "Stages of Grief".

It is also important to note that grief can be anticipatory. In family members of terminally ill patients, this is a major factor leading to complicated grief in bereavement. Anticipatory grief can be defined as a reaction to an imminent and upcoming loss. It may manifest itself when the physical condition of the patient deteriorates and family members are faced with the necessity of final decisions and saying good-byes. I will discuss anticipatory grief in the chapter "Types of Grief".

We will also look at disenfranchised grief (grief that cannot be publicly acknowledged and loss that cannot be publicly mourned). It can be as varied as the loss of a secret lover, losses of partners in gay relationships, or losing a family member convicted of a grave crime.

And, of course, there are situations where grief stops being a normal reaction and begins interfering with the life of the bereaved or starts haunting the grieving person. This is called complicated or pathological grief. It is very difficult to distinguish between normal and pathological grief, and the majority of bereaved people will manage to come to terms with their grief over time. However, there are some people who will experience an extreme overall reaction, persistent symptoms, or an over-intensive manifestation of one of the symptoms of grief.

Why does that happen? Often it is because not all stages of grief have been processed, and because each of us is different and we all react to situations and events in different ways. In the chapter "Types of Grief", I will explain how to know when grief has turned into a complication and when to seek professional help.

Grief is a response to the dissolution of an important bond. The deeper the attachment between the deceased and the bereaved, the stronger the grief reaction can be. Evolutionary scientists often explain grief as the need to maintain important bonds in families, social groups, and communities that we as humans form over the duration of our lives. We will look at some other explanations of the grief experience which have been formed by science in the last few decades. I find that it helps my clients to understand some theories behind grieving, to see how some of the emotions and feelings they are going through can be explained through the lens of scientific knowledge. In the chapter "Types of Grief", I will briefly present some of the major theories that explain grief which I find helpful in my work.

In this book, I share many stories of grief, some of them real written with the permission of my clients and some of them fictional, inspired by the real life stories I witness around me.

I am very grateful to the clients who have shared their stories with me. They must remain anonymous, but I acknowledge that this book could not have appeared without them. All the names (and most details of their stories) have been disguised to preserve confidentiality. The emotions, though, remain intact and all stories reveal the extensive work that the bereaved had to go through to enable them to come to terms with guilt, self-reproach, and the pain of grief.

CHAPTER TWO

Myths and Truths About Grief

"While grief is fresh, every attempt to divert
only irritates. You must wait till it be digested,
and then amusement will dissipate the
remains of it."
- Samuel Johnson (1709-1784)

The death of a loved one always brings
sadness and overwhelming feelings of loss,
loneliness, and despair. Before we proceed, I
would like to explain a few terms used in this
book, which are often confusing. *Bereavement*
refers to the *loss* of a loved one. *Grief* is a
reaction to bereavement: a severe and prolonged
distress in response to the loss of an emotionally
significant figure which may manifest itself in
psychological and physical symptoms. Grief is
what you feel inside. *Mourning* is what you show
outside, it is the external display of grief.
Mourning is crying in public, wearing black

clothes (common for widows and other close relatives, in many cultures), and avoiding events.

But if someone does not mourn their loss publicly, doesn't cry, or doesn't want to talk, this does not mean that the person doesn't experience grief. What you show and what you feel can be two different things. Grief will usually present itself through psychological and physical symptoms. I emphasize, again, that many feelings of grief may be hidden, and a grieving person may only share a part of what they feel inside.

Symptoms of grief can be divided into affective, behavioral, cognitive, and physiological (or somatic) manifestations.

Affective symptoms may include depression, despair, anxiety, guilt, anger, disbelief, numbness, shock, panic, sadness, anhedonia (loss of ability to enjoy pleasurable activities), and feelings of isolation and loneliness.

Behavioral symptoms may include agitation, fatigue, crying, change in social activities, absent-mindedness, social withdrawal, or seeking solitude.

Cognitive symptoms may include preoccupation with thoughts of the deceased, lowered self-esteem, self-reproach, helplessness and hopelessness, inability to believe in the loss, and problems with memory and concentration.

Physiological symptoms may include loss of appetite, sleep disturbances (feeling lethargic or not being able to sleep through the night), loss of energy and exhaustion, physical complaints similar to those the deceased had endured when alive, drug abuse, and susceptibility to illness and disease.

Grief may also lead to spiritual emptiness and pessimism.

Grief symptoms can be overwhelming and distressing. However, it is important to accept them and not avoid them. It is helpful to keep in mind that all of your symptoms and reactions are common and natural, and that you are not alone.

Grief as a reaction to an immediate loss can present itself in two forms. The first one is protest, defined as a preoccupation with loss, the feeling of pain, agitation, and tension, and accepting the possibility that the deceased may reappear. The second is despair, defined as the opposite of protest and characterized by depression, persistent sadness, and a withdrawal of attention from real life. Protest and despair may come and go in phases. Often protest sets in first and then despair takes over. In both the protest and despair states, feelings of guilt, anger, and anxiety are present and are experienced by grieving individuals.

Grief symptoms may be different, depending on the type of loss. For example, the loss of a spouse awakens feelings of loneliness and abandonment, while the loss of a child evokes feelings of having failed to protect the child, and self-blame. We will look at the differences in grief, depending on the type of loss, in further chapters.

Grief has been described as an emotion; however, it is currently being regarded more and more as a disease. As this trend continues, grief will accrue more and more definitions particular to disease and will lose the definition of being an emotion.

Earlier research provides solid evidence of biological links between grief and an increased risk of illness and mortality. Bereaved individuals are at higher risk for depression, anxiety, and other psychiatric conditions, and are highly susceptible to infections and a variety of other physical illness due to a considerable weakening of the immune system. Bereaved individuals have higher consultation rates with doctors, use more medication, and are more often hospitalized. An increased risk of mortality and suicide is associated with medical conditions in bereavement.

Needless to say, people in grief will neglect their own health by not maintaining a well-balanced diet, forgetting to take necessary medications, not getting enough sleep, and not exercising. Some may abuse alcohol, smoke excessively, use drugs, or engage in other self-destructive behaviors.

Social support is very important in grief. However, a grieving person should be advised to designate their own comfortable boundaries of support (for example, by telling people what exactly they can do to help them, when, and for how long they would like to be together, or sharing that they may not want to do certain activities now, but would consider doing them later).

Finally, the grief process may be different for every individual. It is important for the bereaved to do as they feel, especially during the mourning phase: to be left alone if they so wish, or allowed to cry or to have a chance to talk to someone when they feel the need. It may be helpful to engage in activities that help commemorate their loved one: for example, through attending religious services, visiting the gravesite, praying, creating a memory book with photos and stories, or assembling a memory box with the belongings of the deceased, or by giving to a good cause such as medical research, a scholarship fund, or charity.

Grief is often compared to Post Traumatic Stress Disorder (PTSD), particularly in the acute phase of traumatic grief, which holds similar symptoms such as re-experiencing, avoidance-numbing, increased arousal, guilt, shame, changes in value systems and beliefs, and a search for meaning. Often, in traumatic grief, the relatives of the deceased are preoccupied with issues surrounding the trauma such as the pain of dying, the cause of death, and self-blame for not being able to protect/save or for having survived. Traumatic images flood the consciousness of survivors.

In grief, it is important to resolve feelings of guilt, anger, anxiety, and depression. Sadness occurs both in depression and grief. The difference is that in grief, sadness is focused on missing the person who died, while in depression, sadness is focused on hopelessness and helplessness about self, the world, and the future. Sadness is normal in grief; however, depression in a time of grief can make it very difficult to come to terms with loss and reconstruct a life going forward.

There are a lot of examples of unhelpful thinking that can block the normal bereavement process and cause emotional distress. Negative thinking can lead to the symptoms of complicated grief and depression. For example, self-blame or self-reproach can heavily impact the emotional condition of the bereaved.

In overcoming the pain of grief, it is critical to consider what is causing self-blame and other negative thinking about self, the world, life, the future, and what causes anxious and depressive avoidance behavior. Often patients with complicated grief continue to perceive their loss as "unreal" or remain preoccupied with thoughts and recollections of the deceased or the death event. Working through grief in therapy helps patients change the perception of loss into something more "real", helps them to acknowledge their loss, and ensures the loss is recognized as permanent and not reversible. Unless this is done, thoughts of the deceased will constantly bring fresh emotional distress and sorrow.

Let's look at some myths and negative thoughts that may be obstacles to recovery, and consider how to handle them.

Myths about Grief

"Give sorrow words; the grief that does not speak knits up the o-er wrought heart and bids it break."
— William Shakespeare, *Macbeth* (1564-1616)

There are many beliefs in the culture and traditions of different people about how to deal with death and grief. Many traditions are passed on to us through generations and we follow them without questioning the reasons behind them. Indeed, it is not easy to change the long-held beliefs of our families or to insist on doing things differently. But holding on to archaic knowledge at a time when we have gained so much understanding about the subject from research and therapy would be wrong. It is in the best interest of each of us - our families, loved ones, and society as whole - to embrace this new knowledge and dispel the myths that still govern our societies and often cause harm to people.

Some of the common myths I often hear are:

All losses are the same

No loss is equal. There are many different factors that affect grief. Grief varies between young and old, between cultures and religions, and depends on the type of relationship the bereaved had with the deceased (parent, child, spouse, sibling, grandparent, friend, lover), the levels of existing dysfunction, and upon the nature of death (if the death was expected or sudden). It depends on previous experiences with death and on the attachment style, and of course, interpersonal factors play a very important role. It depends on the personality of the bereaved, as well. Unprocessed emotions in that relationship, conflicts, repressed feelings, unspoken words: all these all come out in grief and weigh heavily on the grieving person, thus complicating recovery.

Mourning should last for a year

There can be no exact time frame for grief or mourning. As every loss is different, it will take every person a different amount of time to come to terms with their loss. Different cultures also may have their own rules on mourning (i.e. widows required to wear black for several months, a year, or a lifetime, or are prohibited to re-marry, and so on). Irrespective of all rules, every person will ache differently, will go through their memories of the deceased on their own terms, will arrive at forgiveness for him/herself and the deceased, and will find their own meaning in continuing to live.

Once you get over your grief, it never comes back

Stages of grief known as denial, anger, bargaining, depression, and acceptance may come and go in sequence and interchangeably. The duration and intensity of each stage may vary greatly. The stages can overlap or occur together, and a grieving individual can miss one or more stages altogether. It is also not rare for someone to go back and forth between the stages, as important pieces of information about the nature and causes of death come to light. New cycles of grief can be launched at milestone birthdays or anniversaries of the deceased or the bereaved person, and during major family events (the birth of children, the death of other family members, a family relocation, or the sale of the house where the deceased lived, for example).

It is better to avoid anything that reminds you of the deceased

Avoidance is the worst coping strategy in grief outside of denial. Even the most painful reality is better dealt with head on and with full realization of what has happened. Avoiding reminders of the deceased and denying a loved one's death will only extend the time needed to come to terms with the loss and achieve acceptance. Denial and avoidance may come naturally as the first reaction to the shocking news; however, it should not last too long, as a healthy coping pattern requires that the grieving person should work through their pain and loss to restructure their perceptions to help themselves emerge from grief. Grief also comes in cycles, so it is normal to try and avoid reminders of the deceased loved one during these periods of intense longing. However, it is more helpful to dedicate a space and time in your life to purposefully embrace what seems to cause pain (photographs, personal belongings, letters) and celebrate the presence of the lost loved one in your life.

Feeling angry while grieving is not right

Anger is one of the healthy and normal feelings of grief. In fact, anger constitutes one of the five stages of grieving (denial, anger, bargaining, depression, acceptance). Anger is the first realization that the loss is real. Anger comes when the bereaved starts looking for something or someone to blame for the loss. It can revolve around the feeling of guilt for not protecting a loved one or not being there when they died. It is helpful to understand that anger in grief is not similar to anger in ordinary daily life. The cause of this anger can't be undone: no one can make it right. Anger in grief is not directed at anyone in particular; therefore, it can involve anyone around the grieving person and even the grieving person him/herself.

Children need to be protected from death, funerals, and grief: they can't understand it, anyway

Children at different developmental stages understand death, dying, and loss differently. However, as they mature, they often question the information previously received. Honest and clear explanations appropriate for the age of the child will help a child deal with loss and help them form a trusting relationship with the surviving significant adult. The child learns how to grieve by looking at parents, other family members, or significant adults in life. The way the child grieves the first loss and the coping mechanism and skills they learn while living through this loss will remain with them for life. If a child is shielded from any contact with pain, loss, and grief or is told fairy tales about what happened, he/she will form mental misrepresentations and misperceptions of reality that will block healthy and reasonable thinking and may become a foundation for future fears and phobias.

You can't continue a relationship or communicate with your loved one after they die

Death ends a life, but does not end a relationship. Everyone who goes through the loss of a loved one will realize this. Relationships with a loved one carry on and continue for as long as they are remembered. The heritage of a person is formed through memories, photographs, and recalling the sayings, deeds, and impact your loved one had on your life. Many bereaved people report mentally talking to the deceased. When a very close person is lost, you would know how he/she would react to events happening in your life after the loss, what they would say, and what advice they could have given you. An ongoing mental connection with the deceased proves the strength of the bond that existed and allows the bereaved to feel the connection and existence of the deceased in their life.

The intensity of your mourning and grieving proves how deeply you loved the deceased

The intensity of grief and the intensity of mourning are not the same things. Grief is your internal reaction to the loss and mourning is the external display of grief. Very often, these two do not coincide. As we know, people often differ in how they express their emotions, depending on whether they are extroverts or introverts, on how close, understood, and accepted they feel in their social circle, and on many other factors. So if someone is not mourning their loss publicly, doesn't cry, and doesn't want to talk, it does not mean that the person doesn't experience grief. What you show and what you feel can vary a lot. This is particularly true for children and adolescents who often have difficulty expressing their feelings in public, fearing judgment or feeling uncertain about how to do so simply because they have still not reached their emotional maturity.

People who have physical problems in grief must have been sick before

Grief causes many different symptoms affecting the psychological, behavioral, and physiological health of the bereaved. Physiological symptoms may include loss of appetite, sleep disturbances (feeling lethargic or not being able to sleep through the night), loss of energy and exhaustion, physical complaints similar to those the deceased had endured, drug abuse, and susceptibility to illness and disease. Previously healthy individuals may present with severely weakened health during and as a result of their bereavement. Through research in the last decades, we now know that grief is associated with an increased risk of illness, the most common being infections due to the weakening of the immune system as well as depression, anxiety, and other psychiatric conditions. Bereaved individuals are more likely to seek medical help as both outpatients and inpatients, and may use more medication. A grieving person will usually neglect his/her own health by not maintaining a well-balanced diet, forgetting to take necessary medications, not getting enough sleep, and not exercising. Some may abuse alcohol, smoke excessively, use drugs, or engage in other self-destructive behaviors.

Funerals and rituals are socially required: they play no role in accepting death or helping us heal

Cultural and religious traditions in memorial services and funeral arrangements serve a great purpose of providing a safe and calming environment allowing the relatives and friends of the deceased to mourn their loss. They instill order in the face of shock and overwhelming pain and serve as an important step in the process of grieving. The denial of loss will usually be resolved after the funeral, as obvious facts of saying good byes and burying the body make the reality of loss hard to avoid. And finally, even though we don't like doing things that are socially required, knowing that the memorial service was attended by all those close to the deceased and the family of the deceased, who expressed condolences and grieved together with the family, also provides a soothing effect of knowing a family is not alone in its grief. The family also finds comfort in knowing that the deceased would have approved of the ceremony held in his/her memory and would have been touched by such an outpouring of kind words and memories and the support for his/her loved ones.

If you are a strong person, you will keep yourself collected, in control, and not show how upset you are by crying. Crying doesn't help.

The days are long gone when crying in public or displaying emotions was considered to be embarrassing or a sign of weakness. Today we know that even the strongest of us cry: it takes strength to express emotions, and crying holds a therapeutic effect by relieving the pressure of internal pain and releasing it through tears. Cry if you feel like crying, and don't hold back. Crying is healing, revealing that you are human, too, and that your heart is not made of stone. Allow yourself the luxury of being weak when being strong serves no purpose. Crying helps, and should never be considered a sign of weakness.

You will cry, mourning the loss of a very special person in your life: but remember that its the life that was lost; not the relationship. Your relationship with the person will continue no matter what, through memories and keeping that person in your heart.

You may mourn the loss of your hopes for the future with this person, but remember that you can go on in the future and do things you were planning to do together in the memory of your loved one.

Going on with your life means putting behind you the memories of your loved one and your life together

"Moving on with your life" means processing loss and focusing on major tasks that need to be completed in order to emerge from grief. These include accepting the reality of a changed world, taking time off from the pain of grief, adjusting to a world that doesn't include the deceased, and developing a different connection with the deceased while embarking on a new life. The deceased will not (and should not) be forgotten in order to emerge from grief. Quite the contrary: incorporating loss and memories of the loved one into one's new life after loss helps grievers move on. It may be helpful to remember the deceased by engaging in activities that help commemorate a loved one. Examples include attending religious services, visiting the gravesite, praying, creating a memory book with photos and stories, or assembling a memory box with the belongings of the deceased, or giving to a good cause such as medical research, a scholarship fund, or charity.

You need to keep yourself busy and distract yourself with other activities, rather than actively grieve your loss

Grief is a process that requires a lot of work from the bereaved. Avoiding dealing with grief will only extend a cycle that needs to be completed in order to emerge from grief. Take time to grieve your loss, and don't be hard on yourself. The grief process may turn into a roller coaster with many ups and downs if you don't process and come to terms with your feelings. The feelings you will experience are yours and yours alone. They are neither right nor wrong; they just need to be respected, expressed, and acknowledged.

I could continue this list, but I think you understand that most things that we hear when someone passes away are dysfunctional and negative beliefs that often dictate our behaviors and lead to a worsening of bereavement in grief. I hope that, with time, these negative beliefs can be left in the past where they rightly belong.

How to Help Yourself in Grief

> "Only people who are capable of loving
> strongly can also suffer great sorrow, but this
> same necessity of loving serves to counteract
> their grief and heals them."
> - Leo Tolstoy (1828-1910)

One of the strongest reasons for writing this book was to provide enough information to put the myths about grief to rest and assure grievers that everything they feel is normal, and that they have a right to behave as they feel. Holding on to myths can hinder the healing process and lead to depression and frustration. It is very important to have realistic expectations of what you may and will experience in grief.

These true expectations are:

Grieving is a natural process
It leads slowly from the pain of loss to a new life without the deceased. You don't get over it: you learn to live with it.

Your grief will change with time

It does not always decrease intensity. The grief process is much more like a roller coaster, with ups and downs happening at times when you least expect them.

You are the expert about your own grief
No one can understand your grief better than you do.

When you grieve, you grieve not only the person you have lost
You also grieve all the hopes and dreams you held for a future with the person who died.

You have the right to your own feelings
No feelings are right or wrong: they just *are,* and you and other people around you need to respect that. Give yourself permission to feel and express all the emotions you are experiencing.

Crying is one of the ways of coping with grief
Tears help us release the pain and pressure from within. Crying doesn't mean that you are weak or cannot control yourself. Tears mean that you have loved. Crying helps you heal. So go ahead and cry.

You will experience physical problems as you grieve

Our immune system is strongly influenced by our emotions. In times of acute stress, our bodies' defenses are focused on restoring emotional and physical balance, and the immune system's ability to fight bacteria, viruses, and cancer cells is impaired. Loss of appetite or overeating, lack of sleep or lethargy, and lack of physical activity are just a few critical symptoms of grief. Therefore, when in grief, it is very important to take care of yourself. Fresh air, walks, rest, physical activity, and good food are essential to keep the body functioning and the immune system strong. Try to stay away from drugs, alcohol, or tranquilizing medications as these can delay your healing. Be good to yourself.

Grief brings despair

You may feel you have nothing to live for. Sometimes you might wish your life would end, to stop the pain. Please remember that you are not alone. Many people feel and think this way, but over time their pain lessened and they found a sense of meaning and went on living. Time may not heal all wounds, but it helps.

You may blame yourself for your mistakes

Some mistakes may be real, while others are imaginary. Talk about your thoughts with others: it helps. Find a therapist who works with grief if you feel that self-blame and guilt are hindering your healing. It is possible to find forgiveness and restructure even the heaviest guilt.

It is normal to feel angry when grieving

You may feel angry at the person who died (or left you alone), at other family members, at doctors or anyone who didn't save your loved one or did not do enough to help, at other families who have not lost their loved ones - even at God and the whole Universe. Releasing your anger and working with it helps you heal. Suppressing anger leads to depression and harms you physically.

The death of a loved one can challenge your beliefs

These beliefs may be in God, in your religion, or in the justice of the Universe. There is nothing wrong with it. Many people find answers in their religion during times of grief: they find a deeper meaning of life, their faith, and overall philosophy.

The loss of your loved one may trigger grief for earlier losses that you had not resolved at the time when they occurred

Unresolved losses, guilt, and self-blame will need to be resolved as part of confronting your current loss. Think of this as a chance to heal your old wounds; to become free from carrying heavy old luggage.

Grief will evoke your own mortality issues and force you to re-evaluate your identity

Give yourself time to process these important aspects. Seek help, if necessary.

Give yourself permission to grieve

Feelings are neither right nor wrong, they need to be respected, expressed, and acknowledged.

What Not to Say to a Grieving Person

"Is it really possible to tell someone else what one feels?"
- Leo Tolstoy, *Anna Karenina* (1828-1910)

Many grieving individuals are even more hurt by the sayings and meaningless phrases that are commonly said to someone who has lost a loved one. One of the most common is "I know how you feel, my mom/dad/cousin/friend died last year…". However, comparing tragedies and losses is never helpful. It is NOT what a grieving person needs to hear at the time of loss.

Below is a list of hurtful and damaging sayings that bring no relief to a grieving person. Some people don't even know why they say those things. Often the situation is awkward, and these words come to mind because we heard them from others, or heard our parents saying them in response to loss. Most of these sayings refer to getting over the loss quickly and offer advice on how to avoid the pain. But as I explain in this book, avoiding the pain and skipping the grieving stages (or going through them too quickly) is not a realistic expectation.

Trying to avoid the pain or reminders of loss is unhelpful, will backfire at a later stage, and will only cause more pain and destruction. Please consider avoiding common platitudes and "click phrases" and think about offering more thoughtful and meaningful support to a grieving person.

Platitudes and sayings to avoid include:

1. I know how you feel.
2. God has a plan for all of us.
3. Just look at all the things you have to be thankful for.
4. He is in a better place now.
5. God needed another angel.
6. At least he is not suffering anymore.
7. She is at peace now.
8. Everything is for the best.
9. Thank God, you/others are still alive. It could have been worse.
10. You still got your other kids/spouse/other parent.
11. Don't cry... it will not change what happened, and will only upset you.

12. This, too, will pass.

13. He lived a full life.

14. God never gives you more than you can handle.

15. You need to get on with your life.

16. You are strong, you can handle this.

17. You must be strong for the kids/for others.

18. You will get over it in time.

19. Time heals all wounds.

20. In a year everything will be ok.

21. You'll be fine, just give it some time.

22. You are young, you could always have more children.

23. You need to be a man in the house now/you need to take over his/her duties now.

How to Help a Grieving Person

> "You can clutch the past so tightly to your
> chest that it leaves your arms too full to
> embrace the present."
> — Jan Glidewell (1944-2013)

When you find yourself next to a grieving person, do not be afraid. The death of a loved one is a natural event in life, and can happen to any of us. There are some basic rules on what to do and say. As we discussed, many of them will depend on the stage of grief a person is going through and the type of loss experienced. Here are some common tips on what to do or say to help someone in grief.

Be present

Just be there. Give the grieving person a hug or a kiss, hold their hand, and offer them a shoulder to cry on. Say "I'm sorry", "I am here for you", "I care". Even if you don't know what to say, your presence provides comfort, and so is helpful.

Acknowledge the loss in an honest way

Do not avoid the words "died" or "killed", and do not substitute them for euphemisms like "passed away". Say "I heard that your father died. I am so sorry for your loss".

Make your presence felt by offering practical help

Do not say "Call me if there is anything I can do". Instead, say "I'm going shopping. I can bring you bread, milk, or fruits. Is there anything else you need from the store?" Volunteer to take the children to school or take care of them at your house. Come and make lunch, or help with laundry and water plants. Make your presence felt.

Make tea or coffee, sit down with the grieving person, and listen

Let the grieving person talk when they are ready. Don't ask how they feel and don't tell them how they should feel or what they should do. Instead, say: "Would you like to talk?", or just listen. This is what is needed most at this moment: quiet support.

Don't say or pretend that you know how they feel

The truth is, you don't. Comparing losses and tragedies is never helpful. Don't pity the grieving person, but do express sympathy. Being next to the grieving person can make us feel helpless and awkward. It is better if you are honest and say: "I am not sure what to say to you or how to help you, but I want you to know I care. I am so sorry for your loss".

Often, the grieving person will ask: "Why?"

This is not a question, but an expression of pain. You can't answer that either, so simply reply: "I don't know".

Do not use formulated statements

Statements like "It's all in God's hands" or "It is God's will" or "You will be alright soon" are not helpful. They can't console, they sound fake, and they can be alienating. Better say nothing or offer a hug instead.

There is no schedule for grieving

There is no timeframe of how long the mourning and grieving will take. Be patient. Stand by the grieving person. Be there to listen to them. Share fond memories of the deceased. Most grieving people will find relief by talking about the deceased, and they love to hear stories about their lost one. Do not try to change the subject, but encourage these conversations. They are truly healing.

Respect all feelings the grieving person expresses

Encourage them to cry or vent out anger. Never say "You shouldn't feel like that". Feelings are neither right nor wrong: they need to be respected, expressed, and acknowledged.

Remember: a grieving person may have low self-esteem and may blame themselves

This blame may apply for events leading to the death or for their relationship with the deceased. Encourage them to discuss this.

Help the grieving person take good care of themselves

Cook and eat together, go for walks, and encourage exercise. Rest, diet, and exercise are critical to restoring physical and mental well-being.

Do not offer tranquilizers or sleeping aids without a doctor's advice

Much like alcohol and drugs, they may offer temporary relief, but will usually only hinder the healing process.

Negative Thoughts in Grief

"You cannot prevent the birds of sorrow from
flying over your head, but you can prevent
them from building nests in your hair".
- Old Chinese Proverb

Negative thoughts in the form of self-talk are endless stream of thoughts that run through your head every day, in grief. We often refer to this process as automatic thinking.

Automatic thoughts may be positive or negative. Some may be based on logic and reason, while others may be misconceptions formulated from a lack of adequate information or from distorted information. In grief, many thoughts are negative, formed by guilt and self-blame. In order to win the battle with negative thoughts, one has to weed out misconceptions and challenge them with rational and positive thoughts.

Here are some common forms of irrational thinking in grief. I encourage you to identify and challenge these types of thoughts.

Counterfactual Fallacy: "Death Could Have Been Prevented"

Counterfactual fallacy is defined as confusion between "what might have been the case" and "what ought to have been the case". If a griever believes that the negative outcome could have been prevented, he or she may also believe that they should have done something to prevent it; even though, in reality, they had no powers of foresight. Counterfactual fallacy can thus affect both the judgments of others and self-judgments, generating many negative, self-directed affective responses. To handle this type of negative thinking, it is important to acknowledge it - in other words: to understand that you are indeed thinking like this. Then you need to re-examine your beliefs, find irrational patterns, and discourage yourself from using this approach.

It's also important to understand the distinction between characterological and behavioral self-blame. Characterological self-blame is a persistent, distorted, and negative perception of self, experience, and the future that is present in clinical depression, while behavioral self-blame is a more benign affective disturbance without cognitive bias which leads an individual to appraise events and draw logical, helpful conclusions.

In therapy, I focus on distinguishing between characterological self-blame and behavioral self-blame, and I explain how self-blame can become enduring and destructive to personality characteristics. This can help the client shift guilt to a more adaptive (and less destructive) behavioral self-blame. However, most importantly, this helps clients avoid drawing fast counterfactual conclusions without exploring all the available information in a cognitively reasonable manner.

Hindsight Bias: "I Knew Something Bad Was Going to Happen That Day"

Hindsight bias is defined as the individual's belief that they could have predicted the outcome of the event (foresight) based on a knowledge of the outcome (hindsight). In the event of an accident, a common hindsight bias is "knowing that something bad was going to happen that day" or recalling signs and signals that should have indicated an upcoming danger. Hindsight bias generates thinking errors and prevents adaptive learning, as events perceived as inevitable and predetermined do not allow for the influence of other factors. This faulty thinking process increases causal inference errors and self-blame, as the person experiencing hindsight bias is likely to inflate or distort the importance of his/her role. If outcome knowledge was available, the individual would condemn his/her inability to prevent the negative event.

There is a three-step intervention strategy involved in dealing with hindsight bias. First, the therapist explains the definition and concept of hindsight bias to the client, providing appropriate examples. Second, the therapist identifies the magnitude of the faulty thinking and belief that the client could have known what was going to happen before possibly having access to such information. Third, in order to help a client re-examine the event with a more objective assessment of their role (and thus reduce self-blame), the therapist helps them to recognize hindsight bias and to acknowledge the impossibility of knowing the post-outcome data. Clients are also encouraged to learn and change unhelpful "should have" or "could have" statements, identifying them as potentially hindsight-biased and counter-effective.

Counterfactual Thinking: "If Only...Then..."

Counterfactual thinking involves generating imagined alternatives to actual events. It is a mental exercise allowing the individual to undo, change, or rework the facts to arrive at a new outcome. The process is often described by reflections of "if only...then...". Counterfactual thinking may be directed upward or downward. An upward direction is defined by suggesting alternative sequences of events which improve reality; for example: "If I had done this, things would have been better now". Downward direction is defined by connecting the event with a worse outcome; for example: "It could have been much worse". Upward counterfactual thinking leads to negative emotional consequences, while downward counterfactual thinking leads to an improved emotional reaction to trauma and stressful events.

Counterfactual thinking and the relation of upward and downward directions of counterfactuals can be explained through Festinger's social comparison theory. This theory suggests that individuals have a tendency to evaluate themselves in comparison with others. Therefore, the downward social comparison with a less able, less attractive or less powerful individual enhances one's self-esteem and vice versa, where an upward social comparison with a more able, more attractive, or more powerful individual is ego-deflating.

Counterfactual thinking is generated mostly in cases where events involve a negative, unexpected, or unwanted outcome. The individual then adopts a "if only" mentality. Bereaved parents or spouses who are grieving the death of a loved one in a car accident often have "if only" thoughts years after the accident. The tendency to blame themselves for not preventing the accident is much stronger than the tendency to blame the cause, further worsening the negative emotional state of the bereaved. In contrast, the generation of downward counterfactuals that suggest a worse development of the scenario than the one that actually happened can bring relief, promote self-esteem, and reduce an individual's negative emotional state. Reflecting upon the negative event and suggesting that a worse outcome has been prevented can alleviate depression and lessen the likelihood of a similar misfortune.

Counterfactual thinking also contributes to the induction of feelings of controllability. They intensify the perceptions of personal causation and control, thus reinforcing self-blame and guilt. "If only I had not done this, the event would not have happened" is a very powerful statement often attributing blame to the individual entertaining the thought even when there is no objective causal connection. Although in the time of chaos and shock it may serve a beneficial purpose to identify personal responsibility, which contributes to a perception of controllability and predictability, in cases of complicated grief, self-blame and guilt, these feelings can lead to a person's worsening condition.

Counterfactuals are schemas in the mind through which experience is organized. Thus, they are subject to errors and biases potentially leading to severely distressing consequences. It is important to identify the process of generating counterfactual thoughts and to restructure the dysfunctional influence of implied schemas.

Meaning Making: "I Can Not Find Any Meaning"
In any traumatic or stressful experience, bereaved individuals need to find meaning from the event which they can adapt to changes in their lives. In cases of the death of an elderly

individual, the experience validates our cognitive constructions and assumptions of death being an expected, appropriate conclusion to a long-lived life. However, traumatic deaths and deaths of younger individuals challenge these beliefs.

There are three basic assumptions which are challenged by grief and trauma. The first one is that the world is a benevolent place, the second is that the world is meaningful, and the third is that the self is worthy. In grief and trauma, these assumptions turn into "illusions". The outcome is that the survivor will come to positively perceive the surrounding world and self, and will incorporate the loss into his/her new assumptive world.

Bereaved individuals find it difficult to maintain their old assumptions but, at the same time, cannot entirely accept the new ones; becoming "stuck" between the two which hinders the re-establishment of a meaningful life. Routines for modifying schemas or cognitive representations in one's life will include reordering one's priorities, focusing on reachable goals, and adapting the individual's self-image to that of being a survivor. Reinterpreting the event using a positive focus and comparing one's situation to others who are worse off allows for re-establishing a sense of control through simply accepting the situation and becoming aware that certain efforts to regain control have already been successful.

Individuals who view the surrounding world as malevolent may be helped to develop a more balanced belief system. Changing negative core beliefs requires a guided consideration of the evidence for and against a certain affect-intensive belief, enabling the schema to change.

During the therapy and exploration of the evidence for and against a certain interpretation, alternative and balanced views are encouraged. This is done repeatedly, when extreme perspectives are involved, to allow the patient to acknowledge and consolidate new beliefs into his/her cognition system. In cases of absolute and extreme core beliefs, individuals will employ polar opposites such as a benevolent versus malevolent world, and it helps to shift the patient's evaluation to a midpoint using the "continuum" method which rejects absolute thinking patterns.

Causal Inferences: "I am responsible for this"

Causal inferences contribute to the generation of a faulty sense of personal control, improved adjustment, and future preparedness. Such thinking errors do not allow individuals to recognize the multiple, diverse influences outside of their control that caused the event. The errors also confuse thinking by suggesting that the event could have been prevented and the outcome altered. Causal inference is also the failure to differentiate between "responsibility as accountability" and "responsibility as the power to cause or control the outcome". It is important to understand this difference. For example, parents are accountable for the behavior of their children - however, if a child has an accident at school, the parents did not cause the accident.

There are specific interventions for dealing with the processing of causal inferences. First, the therapist attempts to explain the difference between causality, blame, and foreseeing and "knowingly" causing harm, focusing on the hindsight bias involved. Then a more objective analysis of perceived responsibility follows, which involves listing other people and factors who might have causally contributed to the negative outcome, assigning the percentage of outcome responsibility to each of these people-factors, and then re-examining the client's initial appraisal of their causal contribution.

Filtering: "Focusing only on the negative"

Sometimes the negative aspects of a situation or a relationship can be magnified, filtering out all of the positive ones. In grief, for example, the bereaved often focus on a remaining disagreement with the deceased or an inability to ask for forgiveness or say "I love you", forgetting the positive events in the relationship, the years of happiness, or the many times they helped the deceased or showed the deceased how much they cared.

Personalizing: "It is all my fault"

Personalizing means that when something bad happens, you automatically blame yourself. Personalizing is a variation of counterfactual fallacy thinking and causal inference; however, it is characteristic of a person who tries to control everything and does not recognize that many events in life are beyond our control.

Catastrophizing: "It will end badly"

You automatically anticipate the worst. Years after losing a spouse, the bereaved may refuse to form a new relationship for fear of becoming attached and losing a loved one again. Sometimes one change in a daily routine will lead the person to believe the day will be a disaster.

Polarizing: "White or black"

You see things only as either good or bad, white or black. There is no middle ground. You feel that you have to be perfect or that you are a failure, or that the relationship is either ideal or a failure. These absolute thinking patterns in grief may turn reality into something "absolutely unbearable". It helps to shift the perspective on a continuum, to avoid using extreme descriptions, and to move thinking towards more acceptable median values.

You can learn to deal with negative thoughts. However, the process requires time and practice. Throughout the day, stop and evaluate what you're thinking. Find a way to avoid judging yourself. Start by following one simple rule: Don't say anything to yourself that you wouldn't say to someone else. Be gentle and encouraging. If and when a negative thought enters your mind, evaluate it rationally and respond with affirmations of what constitutes realistic thinking about that situation.

Eventually your self-talk will automatically contain less self-criticism and more self-acceptance. Your spontaneous thoughts will become more positive and rational.

CHAPTER THREE

Stages of Grief

"Every one can master a grief but he that has it."
- William Shakespeare, *Much Ado About Nothing* (1564-1616)

Stages of grieving, as suggested by Elizabeth Kübler-Ross in 1969, are known to many as denial, anger, bargaining, depression, and acceptance. In 1970, Bowlby and Parker suggested that the stages of grieving should be described as numbness, pining, disorganization, and reorganization. Whichever model of separating the stages is examined, it is important to know that the duration and intensity of each stage may vary greatly, that stages can overlap or occur together, and that a grieving individual can miss one or more stages altogether.

It is also not unusual for someone to go back and forth between the stages as important pieces of information about the nature or causes of death, milestone birthdays, anniversaries, and events in the family can newly aggravate grief symptoms and re-launch a grief stage from the past. Getting stuck in a stage or a major variation in the process may be considered pathological and would require a call for action, such as consulting a therapist for help.

Stage 1 – Denial

Loss is always a shock, so the first reaction that follows the death of a loved one is denial of the fact that the loss has occurred. The loss seems unreal. The griever thinks he could turn back time, wake up, and everything will be as it was before the loss. It seems impossible that the person loved and lost could be no more. You know you sound irrational, but you still believe things could go back to how they were before, and that what you lost will return. It may be a way for your brain to shut down in an effort to self-preserve and block the first wave of pain. Thoughts like "He has not died", "She will be back", or "He could not have left me" are common in this stage.

Denial is also associated with isolation, where the grieving person will insist on being left alone and will require time to process what happened. This is absolutely normal. Give the person as much space and time as they need. A couple of days or weeks would be enough for this stage, but watch out if it lasts longer than a month. Make sure the person knows you are there for him or her, if they need to talk or just want "silent company". Suggest that you could go for a walk, drive around, visit the cemetery, or go to church together. Any shared activity could help the grieving person feel that life has not stopped and that they need to process their loss. Usually the stage of denial and isolation ends by itself as the grieving person's mind tapers into the "unsafe" territory of loss and begins to embrace it.

Stage 2 – Anger

After you realize that you have lost something or someone who was dear to you, it is normal to start feeling angry. It is the first realization that the loss is real. When you start looking for something or someone to blame for the loss, you may feel guilty for not protecting your loved one or not being there when they died. Intense emotions enter, and you start to blame everything around you – God, the Universe, your job/or responsibilities that kept you away, doctors, the healthcare system, people who were with the deceased at the time of death – anyone or anything that could have contributed to the death or who, in your opinion, were not "good enough" to save your loved one. Questions come to your mind: "Why me?", "How could this happen to me?", "Why would God not protect me and my loved one?". Anger and rage are normal at this stage; however, anger in grief is not akin to anger in ordinary daily life. The cause of this anger can't be undone: no one can make it right. Anger in grief is not directed at anyone in particular; therefore, it can involve anyone around the grieving person, even the grieving person him/herself.

If you are dealing with someone in the anger stage of grief, let the person vent their emotions, listen to him/her, and do not advise them to calm down or control themselves. Just be there and support them while looking after them to ensure they are safe and are not contemplating hurting themselves or others.

Stage 3 – Bargaining

This stage comes when you start pondering if there was anything that you could have done differently to prevent the loss. You begin reflecting about how things could have been different: "This would not have happened if I did not do this or did not say that" or "If only we had gone to see a doctor earlier". It is a typical cognitive discussion, and in a way it is even helpful in reconstructing the events and causes leading to the death of a loved one. Often such bargaining processes help the grieving person receive approval from those around them, along with the reassurance that they could not have changed what happened, they did all they could, and that the loss was not their fault. This is one of the most critical stages of grieving and requires the most support from others. Listen to the person in the bargaining stage. Let them tell you all of their conditional thoughts, including what they think could or should have happened. Make sure to encourage them to share as much as possible, but do not interrupt them or tell them that their thoughts are irrational. Be gentle, take time to talk about everything, and reassure them that certain events in life are beyond our control. Suggest undertaking some activity that the deceased enjoyed, or always talked about experiencing, in the future. Be there when emotions start pouring out.

Stage 4 – Depression

This stage is really the time to say good-bye. You have exhausted your anger, bargaining has led nowhere, and you realize the lost loved one is not coming back. There is nothing you can do, no one you can blame, and no reasons, excuses, or negotiations that can bring the lost person back. It is the feeling of sadness, of actual irreversible loss, that is embraced during this stage. According to clinical science, depression can be categorized as low mood, insomnia or hypersomnia, fatigue, feelings of guilt, sadness, hopelessness, diminished interest in usual activities, irritability, or lack of concentration. All of these feelings are normal for grief; however, the major difference between grief and depression is that the above symptoms in grief focus on the absence of the loved person, while in depression they focus on one's self and feelings of helplessness or hopelessness about current or future situations.

What can you do when someone close to you is suffering from depression? The first rule is to not tell them that you know how it feels. The truth is – you don't. Everyone carries their own cross, and everyone's sadness is different. The best you can do is be there, silent or talking, and make your presence felt. Cook a meal, make a cup of tea, and take care of the person going through this stage. Ensure that they feel listened to and that they can talk to you about anything. Watch out for suicidal thoughts – you need to get help, in that case. Often you will hear thoughts like "I've lost any meaning in life": acknowledge that, but be firm in reassuring the person that life also can continue with the memory of the late loved one. Ask the grieving person how their loved one would have liked to have seen them at this moment, and what would they have wanted them to do.

Dealing with depression is not an easy task. There are specific chemical processes happening in the brain and body of a depressed person which are difficult to reverse. In depression, the interaction of the endocrine system with the immune and the nervous systems is altered, as neurological processes activated by chronic stress and by depression are similar. During depression, the levels of catecholamines -

serotonin, noradrenaline, dopamine drop, and glutamate - raise.

Depression has been associated with the weakening of the immune system. Depressed individuals suffer from impairments of the sleep cycle such as insomnia, further reinforced by the lack of physical exercise and an alteration of eating patterns. Therefore, the critical task in this stage is to encourage the grieving person to take care of themselves and pay attention to their own health by maintaining a well-balanced diet, taking the necessary medications, getting enough sleep, exercising regularly, and avoiding excessive alcohol, smoking, drugs, or other self-destructive behavior. Exercise is particularly important as it helps restore the chemical balance in a person's brain by adjusting the levels of neurotransmitters and hormones.

Stage 5 – Acceptance

This stage is the trickiest stage of all. People may think they have accepted their loss, when really they haven't. In fact, every big milestone and every major event in life will trigger grief again, over and over. This is normal, as it is hard (or even impossible) to accept that someone so important and dear to you is gone. Some people will claim that they have accepted the loss immediately after their loved one has passed away, while others will come to this stage only after passing through all the other stages first. No matter what the timing, the real manifestation of acceptance is the calmness a grieving person will experience as they move on with their life, discovering meaning in continued living and finding the strength and motivation to move on.

Acceptance of loss does not mean forgetting the person who passed away or changing your life to avoid any reminders of the loss. Acceptance is more about integrating the loss into your life and moving on while holding onto the heritage of the person you lost and using this as your strength.

Death is a given from the moment we are born. It is the one sure thing that will happen to every one of us, no matter our social position, health status, education, or political values. Grief is strengthened by the realization that we are not immune from death. Awareness of one's mortality is a conscious perception; an anticipation of the inevitable, which human beings often fear to embrace.

Integration of our own and our loved ones' mortality is a very important step in achieving psychological wellness and avoiding living in fear. The time of death is beyond our control, much as the time of birth is beyond our control before we are born. Thus, acceptance is a truly powerful and important stage in the grieving process, allowing the person to grow stronger, value life more, and honor the memories of a lost loved one by continuing this life journey.

CHAPTER FOUR

Types of Grief

Grief Theories

"The risk of love is loss, and the price of loss is
grief - But the pain of grief is only a shadow
when compared with the pain of never risking
love."
- Hilary Stanton Zunin (1951-present)

As I mentioned in the introduction, grief has
been extensively studied through the lens of
scientific theory. Grief is a normal and natural
reaction to the loss experienced by human
beings, and is explained by many theoretical
frameworks. The broad research available to us
today helps explain many of the feelings,
responses, and emotions experienced in grief.

I find it important to talk about research in my
work: it helps my clients by reassuring them that

what they are going through is normal, and that science has observed these experiences and classified them through theoretical foundations for many, many years. Many studies have been carried out using one or more of these theoretical frameworks and provided solid results to confirm theories or suggest new directions in research.

Sigmund Freud viewed grief as a response and a normal defense against the psychological trauma of loss. Freud suggested that grief as a normal reaction to crisis usually does not require intervention and will resolve over time, by itself. However, we should remember that during the time of Freud's life and research, societies lived in a much more connected manner, and families of several generations often lived in one household, providing support to each other. In today's world, where isolation and virtual communication between friends and family members is a norm rather than an exception, dealing with a stressful event such as grief in solitude may be harder than ever before.

The first theory I would like to present here is the transactional theory of stress by Lazarus and Folkman. Grief is a stressful experience and, therefore, can be reviewed through this theory. The transactional theory of stress describes coping with a stressful event as problem-focused or emotion-focused. In grief, individuals may use both coping strategies interchangeably, depending on the process stage. For example, it may be helpful to react emotionally by crying or venting out the anger and despair of mourning before accessing the situation and making plans for restoring one's life, during the adjustment phase.

The second theory I always talk about with my clients is the attachment theory, first defined by John Bowlby. This theory defines grief as a psychological and evolutionary mechanism securing bonds between individuals. The bonds or attachment between individuals secures a survival mechanism and is regulated by the survival instinct. The nature of human infancy requires a long period of care, nurture, and dependency for the survival of infants and young children. The attachment continues further in life by bonds between parents and children and between spouses to create a family and care for the offspring.

Thus, the loss of attachment causes the instinctual response of crying, searching, and clinging to restore the lost bond. In the case of permanent loss (such as death), the instinctual response continues until a griever reconstructs the loss and deals with the emotional distress. Significant bonds continue despite death, though in a different form. Losses of significant loved ones may trigger revaluation of life assumptions about self, the world, and spirituality. Although it's a negative and painful process, it may also open up opportunities for growth.

According to the attachment theory, the attachment bond could express itself in three ways:

Proximity to the attachment figure
An example of this could be the proximity of a child to the parent, which is perceived by the child as being safe from threats. When proximity to the attachment figure is disrupted, the attached person experiences fear and anxiety.

Accessibility of the attachment figure
An example of this could be, again, a child seeking the presence of a parent, which provides a secure base from which the child might more

confidently confront challenge. Disruption of accessibility creates insecurity over being able to deal with life's challenges.

Separation from the attachment figure

This is the most important facet of the attachment theory. Separation from the attachment figure triggers separation anxiety, a state of anxious distress in the child in which the child's energy and attention are directed to regaining proximity to the attachment figure. Irreversible separation from the attachment figure as a result of the death of the attachment figure causes grief and severe distress.

The attachment bond doesn't dissolve and is maintained even after the death of an attachment figure, through the photographs, letters, personal items connected to the deceased. In the attachment bond, one perceives self either as needy or as protective, depending on the nature of the relationship: i.e. the child is needful of the parent, but the parent is protective of the child. In spousal relationships, the roles depend on the personal characteristics and nature of the relationship.

The third theory I use in my work with grief is called the family systems theory. It focuses on how family members construct the meaning of death, and suggests that the shared meaning of death in a family will greatly influence how the family and each individual member will grieve.

A family's death meaning is shaped through generations and encompasses family structure and processes, traditions, and dynamics. Families who perceive the death of a family member as a relief from pain and suffering have a different perception of death than those who perceive a loved one's death as something that should have been prevented.

Family systems theory provides three concepts to explain the family meaning-making process: roles, rules, and boundaries.

Roles define expectations attached to the position of the member in the family. These can be the role of mother or father, but also the peacemaker, the scapegoat, or the family star. When one of the positions becomes vacant through the death of a family member, the family must appoint a new member to fill the void.

Rules define the family's responses, which govern interactions and grief reactions.

Boundaries define the delineation of family elements within and outside of the family environment, and may include separating the family from its environment, separating generations within the family, or separating subgroups within the family. The meaning of death may be different across the separated groups or between surviving members of a particular group.

It is important to adapt family systems theory to a timeline of grief processes by examining each family member affected and the family's processes and dynamics.

Complicated Grief

"Guilt is perhaps the most painful companion
to death."
- Elisabeth Kubler-Ross (1926-2004)

When the process or a part of the grief process fails and grief interferes with relationships and work or severely impacts health, complicated grief may be the culprit. Complicated grief combines the features of depression and post-traumatic stress disorder and requires intervention to resolve. Complicated grief is a prolonged grief disorder with elements of stress response syndrome.

To meet the criteria for complicated grief, the bereaved presents with symptoms of separation distress (such as searching for the deceased and preoccupation with the loss) and traumatic distress (in the form of disbelief, emotional detachment, and bitterness). These symptoms must cause significant impairments in functioning for a minimum of two months to qualify for the diagnosis of complicated grief. Predictors of complicated grief prior to the death of a loved one include previous loss, exposure to trauma, previous psychiatric history, attachment style, and the relationship to the deceased. Factors associated with the death include violent death, the quality of the caregiving or dying experience, a close kinship relationship to the deceased, marital closeness and dependency, and a lack of preparation for death. Research indicates that perceived social support plays a key role after death, along with cognitive appraisals and high distress at the time of death. Avoidance of reminders of the loss contributes to functional impairment after controlling other symptoms of complicated grief.

Recent research indicates that the severity of complicated grief is associated with global negative beliefs about the self, the world, life, and the individual's perception of the future as well as with catastrophic misinterpretations of grief reactions. Maladaptive behaviors of complicated grief contribute to the formation of persistent depressive symptoms. The paradox of complicated grief lies in a persistent feeling that the loss is "unreal", a continuation of the shock state, and with difficulty acknowledging the loss. This is known to happen as a result of the insufficient integration of loss in an individual's existing worldview.

The choice of an intervention for coping with complicated grief and bereavement depends on a variety of factors. For example, age and the level of psychosocial development are important factors to consider. Grief may be different in younger adults versus older adults, and in younger children versus adolescents. It's also important to take cultural, religious, and social factors into consideration. Finally, the nature of the relationship between the deceased and the survivor and the presence of dysfunctional thoughts and biases may help the therapist choose the type of intervention.

Different interventions are based on different theoretical frameworks or concepts. For example, the attachment theory by John Bowlby allows for examining the nature of the attachment style between the deceased and the survivor (e.g., secure, anxious-ambivalent, or avoidant), the attachment to the deceased, and the suddenness of death. According to Bowlby's (1973, 1980) attachment theory, individuals with a "secure attachment style" have positive mental models of being valued and worthy of others' concern, support, and affection. When separated from an attachment figure through death, secure individuals are likely to engage in the same kind of searching behaviors and affective reactions found in infants removed from their mothers.

In fact, secure individuals would, Bowlby hypothesized, experience an intense period of grief (e.g., searching, pining, and attempts to recover the lost object) that would eventually subside as they accepted the reality of their loss. Anxious-ambivalent individuals are fearful of being misunderstood and under-appreciated, lack confidence, and perceive significant others as being undependable and unwilling or unable to commit to long-term, intimate relationships. Bowlby suggested that such individuals would display a more chronic grief pattern with high levels of distress that do not subside over time, eventually turning into ``complicated'' grief; a reaction that essentially becomes a type of depression.

Adults classified with an avoidant attachment style often report being aloof, emotionally distant, and skeptical; and they see significant others as being unreliable or desiring too much intimacy. Bowlby believed that this form of attachment was associated with the so-called "delayed" or "absent" forms of grief - both considered to be abnormal.

Recent research indicates that individuals who reported having a closer attachment to the deceased and who experienced a more sudden loss reported greater levels of grief. Individuals with an anxious-ambivalent attachment style reported greater levels of grief and depression. Physical symptoms of grief were more likely to be reported by those with an avoidant attachment style. Although not predicted, it was also found that individuals with a secure attachment style reported less depression. Perception of the lower self and social desirability or likability was associated with reports of more grief. The passage of time since the death and less education were associated with less depression, while older respondents reported less physical symptoms of grief. Attachment does not always have to disengage: for example, in sibling bereavement there is a need to maintain a continuing bond, as death only ends a life but does not end the relationship.

In contrast, the cognitive theoretical framework states that unhelpful thinking and behavioral patterns block the normal bereavement process and cause emotional problems. Negative cognition thus causes symptoms of grief and depression. Negative basic assumptions and beliefs about self-blame influence the emotional status of the individual. Therefore, cognitive-behavioral interventions attempt to address the maladaptive cognitions and global negative beliefs about the self, the world, life, the future, and catastrophic misinterpretations of grief reactions leading to anxious and depressive avoidance behavior.

Often, patients with complicated grief continue to perceive their loss as "unreal" or remain preoccupied with thoughts and recollections of the deceased and the death event. Cognitive therapy is helpful in changing the perception of loss into something more "real", working towards an acknowledgement of loss, and ensuring the loss is recognized as permanent and not reversible.

Unless this is done, thoughts of the deceased will constantly activate the attachment response through emotional distress and sorrow and result in behavioral searching for the missing loved one. Helping to integrate the loss into the consciousness will deactivate the attachment response and ease complicated grief reactions.

Anticipatory Grief

"If you're going through hell, keep going."
- Winston Churchill (1874-1965)

Anticipatory grief is a reaction to the imminent and upcoming loss of a loved one. In today's world, as we live in times of rapid advances in medicine, new treatments, and high specialization of modern medical facilities, many acute, deadly diseases, while still remaining terminal, offer patients a further extension of life and provide improved quality of life.

Today there is frequently an extended period of time between the diagnosis of a terminal illness and death. It is a priceless gift for every patient and all families, but also a difficult time of realization that the patient's condition may soon deteriorate, requiring final decisions and good-byes. It creates an longer time during which families and the patient experience anticipatory grief. Anticipatory grief leads to depression, as expectation of the inevitable decline and saying good-bye is extremely hard.

Therese A. Rando, a well-known psychologist who contributed a lot to the study of death experiences, defined anticipatory grief as "the phenomenon encompassing the processes of mourning, coping, interaction, planning, and psychosocial reorganization that are stimulated and begin in part in response to the awareness of the impending loss of a loved one."

But do we know if anticipatory grief leads to a shorter and easier grief when the actual death occurs, or otherwise makes it harder for the griever? On the one hand, when both the patient and their loved ones know death from an existing terminal illness is approaching, they have the time to go over last wishes, "complete unfinished business", ask for forgiveness, resolve conflicts, and say their good-byes. It is possible to detach and prepare for a peaceful dying, which may help the grieving person after the actual death. However, witnessing the deterioration of the patient and the suffering and debilitation brought on by the illness may intensify grief in the long run.

It is important to know that both the patient and the family member are experiencing anticipatory grief. In this form of grief, there is pain of losing the past that cannot be repeated, there is pain of losing the present and control of the present as the condition of the terminally ill person deteriorates gradually and progressively, and of course there is pain of losing the future - daily interactions, hopes, dreams, and expectations of a long-term future.

In anticipatory grief, feelings of financial uncertainty and necessary changes in lifestyle for the period of illness and after death are also common factors creating discomfort.

There are variations to anticipatory grief, depending on the type of impending loss and the dying person's condition. It is obviously very hard to cope with the anticipatory grief of young children losing their parents, or the anticipatory grief of parents losing young children. The profound nature of loss and the inability of the parent to protect a child from dying or experiencing death at the young age contribute to this pain and despair.

The anticipatory grief in families of Alzheimer's disease patients depends on the duration of the illness. The loss of cognitive ability and the patient's change of personality and loss of self-sufficiency bring multiple losses to the patient's family. There is no possibility of completing the "unfinished business", or of saying meaningful good-byes. In general, caregivers of Alzheimer's disease patients are at higher risk of complicated grief due to the intensity of caregiver burdens associated with Alzheimer's disease, caregiver burnout, depression, physical, and psychological deterioration.

The anticipatory grief in loved ones of AIDS patients is another difficult area. Similar to Alzheimer's disease, the intensity of anticipatory grief depends on the duration of illness. But in case of AIDS, there is also a strong stigmatization of patients with the disease. The course of HIV/AIDS may alternate between the periods of good health and periods of battles with opportunistic infections, prolonging anticipatory grief. The stigmatization of patients and diminished ability to grieve the impending or actual loss, include grieving the loss of a loved one to AIDS, is a disenfranchised loss - a loss that is not socially recognized.

The five stages of grief suggested by Elisabeth Kübler-Ross, are known to many as denial, anger, bargaining, depression, and acceptance. It is worth noting that in her initial work, the concept of these five stages came from the work and research Elisabeth Kübler-Ross did with terminally ill patients. It was an attempt to understand the experience of dying individuals. Later on, this work was expanded to explain the experience of any major loss, and we apply it extensively to our work with grief today.

Indeed, the first reaction to news of terminal illness diagnosis is shock, denial, and disbelief. "It can't be true" or "Maybe there is a mistake" are common thoughts at this stage. Later, the anger, resentment , anxiety, and fear set in ("How could this happen?"). The next stage is bargaining, where questions "Why me?" and "Why us?" come in. The depression stage is marked by sadness, guilt, feelings of failure, helplessness, and fear of impending loss. Some patients and families may reach the final stage of acceptance described by Elisabeth Kübler-Ross. Some may be stuck in one of the stages, or move interchangeably between the stages. It is not uncommon for denial to be followed by depression, then bargaining and anger, and then denial again.

The work of a psychologist during the difficult period of anticipatory grief is to help patients resolve denial and develop an awareness of actual events, acknowledge the nature of illness and its negative prognosis. The faster that denial can be dispelled, the sooner the griever can move through the other stages, finding comfort and peace. The grief of many losses, following anticipatory grief will last for longer periods of time, going back and forth in stages.

The anticipatory grief period needs to be used to work on and work through any "unfinished business". To prevent the patient and his family from entering a "non-communicative" barrier, it is important to encourage talking about fear of death, loss, and helplessness as well as future plans. The patient should not feel excluded from the dynamics of family life, which will and must go on despite the pain of impending death. Many people faced with anticipatory grief find that holding on to hope is not the same as holding on to the patient. The process of completing the "unfinished business" with the dying person, of letting go, doesn't mean letting go of hope.

Disenfranchised Grief

"Tears are the silent language of grief."
- Voltaire (1694-1778)

Disenfranchised grief is grief that cannot be publicly acknowledged and loss that cannot be publicly mourned. There are a number of reasons why grief may be disenfranchised. It may be the loss of a secret lover, losses of partners in gay relationships, or losses of family members convicted of grave crimes. Society rules dictate that funeral arrangements are undertaken by those of "kin" to the deceased. They are those who are legally entitled to organize the ceremonies and bury the deceased. There is a hierarchy of those kin relatives - spouse, parents, children, siblings, and then all the rest. The other intimate relations of the deceased - kin or "non-kin" - have no saying and are not considered to be "mourners". The right to the funeral ceremony thus justifies the right to grieve.

An inability to mourn the grief and social non-acceptance and non-acknowledgment by family, friends, and society as a whole make disenfranchised grief particularly difficult to cope with. There is no sympathy for the griever, no recognition of the loss, and no understanding that the griever may need some time off work or should be relieved of some social responsibilities.

Hidden grief and hidden sorrow haunt the griever for a much longer time than the socially accepted norm. These feelings turn into the belief that this grief is inappropriate and thus should not be experienced or displayed. Guilt and shame then enter the scene.

The social rules of grief exist in every society, and every society has norms on what behavior is expected and accepted from the griever. These norms also govern who decides on the funeral procedure, who can legitimately mourn the loss (usually a close circle of family), and who should receive support and sympathy from society.

Yet, losses affect many connections outside of the close family circle, and losses are not limited to the losses of family members. There are losses of significant relationships outside of socially legitimate norms and there are divorces, separations, losses of property, and other transitions in life that can cause feelings of grief. Grieving those losses may contradict the socially accepted norms of mourning. The experienced loss is not recognized by others and thus the griever is not recognized as a bereaved and is not publicly vested with the right to grieve or to mourn the loss.

As we discussed already, there are a number of reasons that grief can be considered disenfranchised:

The relationship is not recognized
A relationship may not be recognized when it is not based on kin ties recognized by society. It can be the relationship between lovers, friends, neighbors, foster parents, colleagues, in-laws, stepparents and stepchildren, caregivers, counselors, and roommates (e.g., in nursing homes).

Such relationships may be close and long-standing, but even though these relationships are recognized, mourners may not have full opportunity to publicly grieve. At most, they might be expected to support and assist family members.

Then there are relationships that may not be publicly recognized or socially sanctioned. For example, nontraditional relationships such as extramarital affairs, cohabitation, and homosexual relationships have tenuous public acceptance and limited legal standing, and they face negative sanction within the larger community.

The loss is not acknowledged

In other cases, the loss is not socially defined as significant. Individuals experience many losses, some death-related (such as perinatal loss) or other non-death-related losses (such as divorce, incarceration, the loss of a job or material possessions, or significant change in personality or temperament that may be unacknowledged by others). Some losses may be intangible. For example, a teenager aspiring to a career in sports is cut from a team, or parents discover that a beloved child suffers from a disability or grave disease. Similarly, the loss of reputation because of scandal, gossip, or arrest can be devastating. Even transitions in life can have undercurrents of loss. Aging, for example, leads to constant developmental losses such as the loss of childhood or other losses associated with different points of life.

The griever is not considered capable of grieving

There are situations in which the characteristics of the bereaved in effect disenfranchise their grief. Here, the person is not socially defined as capable of grief, therefore, there is little or no social recognition of his or her sense of loss or need to mourn. Despite evidence to the contrary, both the old and the very young are typically perceived by others as having little comprehension of or reaction to the death of a significant other. Similarly, mentally disabled persons may also be disenfranchised in grief.

The nature of death

The nature of the death may constrain the bereaved from soliciting support and limit the support extended by others. For example, many survivors of a suicide loss often feel a sense of stigma, believing that others may negatively judge the family because of the suicide. Similarly, the stigma of AIDS may lead survivors of an AIDS-related loss to be circumspect in sharing the loss with others.

The characteristics of the deceased

The characteristics of the deceased at the time of death may also impact the bereaved's grieving experience. For example, grieving the death of a serial killer, terrorist, or other criminal convicted of grave crimes, or of a drug addict or AIDS patient, may not be recognized by society as a justifiable reason for mourning. It puts intense pressure on the relatives of the deceased, who may acknowledge the wrong-doings of their loved one while still unconditionally loving him as a child/husband/parent/sibling.

The very notion of disenfranchised grief creates additional problems. In grief, one of the most important factors helping recovery is social support. This is completely lacking in disenfranchised grief. Additionally, the bereaved in disenfranchised grief may be excluded from taking an active role in caring for the dying. Funeral rituals, normally helpful in resolving grief, may not help here. In some cases the bereaved may be excluded from attending, while in other cases they may have no role in planning those rituals or even in deciding whether or not to have them. There is no recognized role in which a grieving individual can claim their right to grieve the loss and receive social support. Grief remains private.

When dealing with disenfranchised grief, it is important to replenish and compensate for the lack of support and empathy. In today's world, some losses disenfranchised by society may be acknowledged within a smaller subculture. For example, the death of a gay lover may not be fully recognized by family or coworkers, but the grieving lover may be recognized and supported within the gay community. Grieving rules are also changing, over time. It was previously unheard of to allow partners in an unmarried cohabiting couple to make decisions about funeral arrangements. But today even unmarried partners are allowed to take charge and are afforded the right to publicly mourn their loss. Thus, society is becoming more supportive of some of the previously disenfranchised losses.

CHAPTER FIVE

Grief in Children

"You can't sit around and wait for the storm to be over. You've got to learn how to dance in the rain."
— Anonymous

Children at different developmental stages grieve differently than adults. It is important to adjust what is said about death, dying, and grief to the correct developmental phase of the child in order to achieve the highest possible understanding from a child. Grief in children may present itself through physical symptoms (sleep difficulties, poor appetite, bedwetting, headaches and other physical complaints), psychological symptoms (distress, separation anxiety, fear of death of other loved ones, guilt, depression, attention deficit), and behavioral symptoms (regression, temper tantrums, loss of interest in usual activities, overdependence, seeking attention, extreme shyness).

Children are also known to re-experience grief as they reach new developmental phases and their understanding of events and their contributing factors changes. The presence of a significant adult in the life of a grieving child and the safe feeling of being in a physically and emotionally stable environment are major factors in helping a child overcome grief.

Children may also find it useful to maintain a mental connection with the person who has died, forming a bond which helps them deal with their grief and recover from their loss. Several stages of development in children are known to be associated with specific death attitudes and reactions to the terminal illness or loss of a loved one.

Death is a devastating and catastrophic loss. It reminds adults (and shows children) that no one is immune from the dangers of this world, and that there are events, illnesses, and actions of others that we cannot control. As much as we would have wanted to, we cannot tell our children that the world around us is safe and fair. There are wars, murders, accidents, and pain and suffer around us. It is impossible to live in a world of imaginary perfection, and both adults and children must realize that painful things happen.

An adult in a child's world is a powerful and wise being who is capable of protecting the child and doing anything. The authority of an adult is unquestionable, to a child's mind. This is the reason why "truths and myths" become so permanently encoded in the minds of children. These "truths" accompany the child into adulthood.

In an effort to protect a child from negative emotions and experiences, adults often disguise the truth about death. However, these efforts may actually turn into harm as realization that truth shared about death is untrue turns into fear and brings many phobias. Children meet death at early stages of their life by watching bugs and insects die, by listening to fairytales where characters die, and by learning that their older relatives die. Continuing education and open communication about death (adjusted to the age of the child) helps children understand what death is and how to fight their fears.

Children differ in their reactions to death. However, it would be wrong to think that children perceive death as do adults. At every developmental stage, children have their own perception of reality and the world around them. Understanding these developmental stages and the associated perception of death at each stage will help parents and close relatives to adjust their communication with the child through questions and events related to death, loss, and grief.

Infants and Toddlers

"Death leaves a heartache no one can heal,
love leaves a memory no one can steal."
— From a headstone in Ireland

Infants (up to 2 years old) have not yet formed an understanding of death, and cannot comprehend what death is. However, separation from a significant person may cause grief and anxiety with their surroundings. In severe cases, infants may go through temporary behavioral and developmental regression. Infants will also be impacted by the grief and distress of their caregiver and may cry, behave angrily, lose appetite, or feeling sadness or nervousness from their caregiver. Interventions to protect infants from distress include maintaining routines and avoiding separation from other significant persons in the infant's life.

A child in this age will require frequent touching and holding to reassure them of the existence of bonds and protection. Actions mean more to a child at this stage than words. Large doses of tender loving care - holding, cuddling, and stroking - will help the child move on from the loss of a primary caregiver.

Preschool children

Preschool children (2-6 years old) at this age see death as temporary and reversible. Their perception of life is half real and half fairy tale; thus, children of this age may have a magical explanation of death, or may believe that their bad thoughts or behaviors killed their loved one. Guilt is very common. If intervention is necessary, it is important to address and correct misperceptions. It is important to explain to them that the loved one who passed away is not coming back.

There is a need for physical contact. Cuddling and stroking provide the security of knowing that protection and care are there for the child. Children at this age are most expressive through play. Imagination is very powerful at this stage: a child may "fly to the Moon", "fight monsters", or "talk to imaginary characters". Most fantasies will be based on something the child has heard or seen, even though it was misunderstood.

A child at this age still has a very "magical" understanding of death. He or she may believe that toys are alive when being played with. Dolls and teddy bears want to eat and have to go to sleep, cars on remote control drive because they are alive, and when they stop they can drive again after the battery has been changed.

So when a loved one dies, the child expects that person to be alive again soon. This literal and limited understanding of death may make their reaction to the news of the death of loved one detached and "a matter of fact".

If the child learns about the death of a parent or other primary caregiver, his worry will mostly be about who will care for him/her. The child may react to the loss with tears, but mostly because of the reactions of others and changes in the household routine, not because of the death itself. Abstract explanations of life after death are beyond the child's understanding and will cause concrete questions - "How will Mum sleep there?", "When can we play again?", or "Can grandma come to my birthday?"

All these questions deserve concrete answers. Death is best explained in concrete physical terms, using simple words. It is important to mention the cause of death ("Her heart stopped, he died of old age, she died in a bad accident", etc.) as well as that death is irreversible ("because he or she died, he or she will not be able to move or talk again").

Children who are raised in families that believe in an afterlife can be told that "we buried the old and broken body in the ground, but the soul - the part of him or her that we loved and that loved us - is now gone to Heaven." It is important to make the distinction between the body and the soul, as children who do not know that may begin associating the cemetery and the grave with Heaven and the afterlife, and naturally fear it.

Another common mistake is to say that the deceased has gone to Heaven and now lives there, without mentioning that the body was buried. A grieving child may then wish to go where his or her deceased loved one has moved to. The mind of the child at this age can more easily accept the description of the death and why the body has to be buried rather than the well-meaning but confusing presentation that the loved one is now living elsewhere.

Another possible consequence of a death presentation as a "move to Heaven or elsewhere" is that the child may come to the conclusion that their loved one left because the child was behaving badly. At this age, a child's mind interprets good behaviors as those that are rewarded and bad behaviors as those that are punished. Abandonment by a loved one may feel like punishment to a child. It is also important to point out to the child that their loved one did not choose to die and leave them, and that their death was a result of a severe illness, old age, or someone's reckless behavior.

A child's grief may manifest itself through extreme sadness. A child at this age may regress in a previously-mastered behavior: for example, by bed-wetting or crying upon separation from the remaining parent or caregiver. This is a way of demonstrating the need to be cared for, and should be handled gently, without reproach. Another common reaction to grief is anger and aggression. During play, the child may associate death with a bad monster who comes and hits the doll, the teddy bear, the robot, or the toy car.

Playing with a child and altering the play scenario into a more desirable outcome is the best way to distract the child from sadness, help him express feelings of loss, and enhance his positive, happy outlook on life in general and acknowledge the changed family dynamics.

School age children

School age children (6–8 years old) at this age begin to understand that death is real, final, permanent, and irreversible; however, they do not consider death to be universal or applicable to themselves. Children at this age may express anger towards the deceased or towards those individuals whom they consider guilty of not having saved the deceased.

At this age, children begin to relate to and identify with their peers, gaining information on death and dying from outside the family circle. Magical thinking still plays a role in their games and understanding of life events. At this age, children begin to act more clearly and can verbally express feelings of joy, sadness, and anger. Grief may be expressed through anxiety, depressive symptoms, and feeling unwell. The child may become preoccupied by a fear of death and with safety concerns because they realize, for the first time in their lives, that death is real. No matter what loss they come across at that age, children will feel worried about the possibility of losing a parent or dying themselves. Death looks like an enemy that they are helpless against. As the understanding that death is real sets in, questions about what happens after death arise.

Not all answers can be understood, though, and information needs to be presented in a focused, clear way. Why the person died, what caused the death, and how the death occurred are all pieces of the puzzle a child will seek.

For example, if death occurred as a result of a "drunk driving" accident, the best way to address all questions is to have a discussion on how alcohol and drugs may impair a driver's ability to control themselves, their reactions, and the vehicle they are driving. The child will feel relieved to have his/her anger directed at the person responsible for the accident and will then not continue searching for other explanations of death.

If death occurred as a result of old age, explain that there is nobody and nothing to blame: the human body wears out when it becomes old, much like the old furniture, toys, and clothes, and cannot function as well as it used to. So death from old age is natural. If the death occurred as a result of the illness of a younger person, discuss how many more people died in olden times due to diseases that are easily treatable today (plague, tuberculosis, mumps, chicken pox, rubella), how medicine is constantly evolving to treat diseases that may not be 100% treatable today (like cancer), and how screening for and preventing illness is important. Express sadness that the person who died couldn't be cured from his/her illness, but reflect on how his/her life was extended due to the efforts of doctors, his/her own determination to fight, and modern medicines that would not have been possible 30-50 years ago.

Helping a child of an early school age cope with death should include the provision of clear, realistic information. Children may be invited to participate in the funeral ceremony. Schools must be notified to help teachers monitor the child and provide support.

Pre-adolescents

Pre-adolescents (8–12 years old) at this age develop a more adult understanding of life and death. This understanding includes the fact that plants, animals and people live and die, and that death is irreversible, final, and universal for all living creatures. Pre-adolescents begin to understand the biological aspects and causes of death. However, dealing with feelings is very difficult at this age, and meanings and values cannot be fully appreciated. The child will know that something has happened that cannot be fully understood or explained. Their normal curiosity will be attracted to the physical details of dying, how adults view and react to death, and to cultural traditions and rituals following death.

An attention to the feelings of others will reveal to the child what the loss means to them. As a result, they will learn to empathize others in their sadness and sorrow. While trying to comfort a child who has lost a loved one, allow him or her to take an active part of comforting others. By reaching out and supporting others, the child will be helped to talk through his/her own feelings and can deal with pain.

Often, pre-adolescents will experience feelings of guilt regarding their role in the death. As children grow up and at times when they feel upset with their parents or siblings, they may fantasize about "killing" them (more in a magical way, of course). However, these dreams and fantasies may become haunting as the child starts to believe that their "death wish" for the parent or sibling actually came true and caused the death.

Guilt in a child may be more severe than in an adult, as children cannot utilize all the cognitive reasoning the adult can to come up with enough realistic evidence to overthrow the faulty guilt belief and assure themselves of their innocence. Often children of this age also associate death with punishment for naughty or improper behavior. It is important to identify if guilt is present and, if so, address that by reinforcing again and again that nothing that they did, said or thought could have caused the death.

Children of this age may also resist sharing emotions regarding the death of a loved one. It is difficult for a child to feel different from other children and, therefore, the child may feel ashamed and confused about the loss and how to share it with others. To help the child identify and share emotions, it is helpful to talk about your own emotions and ask the child to share his/her views or feelings. If the child expresses a wish to see the dying patient or to participate in the funeral ceremony, he/she should be allowed to do so, provided an adult takes additional time to share and discuss emotions, feelings, and experiences.

Adolescents

Adolescents (12–18 years old) Girls mature faster than boys, and therefore can be considered adolescents earlier, starting with the ages of ten to twelve. Adolescents understand death as adults. Within their developmental patterns, adolescents fight for their independence, question norms and rituals, and feel that they are not understood by the adults in their life. They live in a world of self-discovery, become self-centered, and relate to everything around them by measuring it up to themselves and their identity, and are very sensitive to peer pressure. At this age, adolescents begin disengaging from family and bond tighter with peers. Although they have strong emotional reactions to death and loss, they usually have difficulty sharing feelings as they face their own social and emotional immaturity.

Teenagers often go through stormy adolescence, rejecting parental standards and established rules. When a parent or a sibling dies, the teenagers' rejection of parental rules and standards turns into extreme guilt. Grief-related guilt may impact school performance.

Being self-centered in adolescence, teenagers may experience stronger fear, guilt, anxiety, and anger in grief than adults. They may think that nobody around is able to have the deep and powerful feelings that they feel, or experiences the excruciating pain that they do. No one has ever loved or grieved like they do. This "superiority belief" may turn into anger and rage, which will express itself in aggressive behavior.

The death of others will turn a teenager's thoughts toward their own death and mortality.

Adolescents question existential beliefs about death and may engage in high-risk activities in an effort to challenge their own mortality. Adolescents feel insecure when they think of death. Most of the time, the high-risk activities and self-destructive behaviors (such as alcohol or drug abuse) are a means of saying "I am not afraid of death". What the adolescent really wants to say is: "I am so afraid of death, I am trying to control my fear and insecurity by turning it into a game." Extreme activities, a lack of focus on reality, and loud music in the background are each a means of escaping from fears.

Interventions in adolescence must support independence and the strengthening of social ties with classmates and friends; however, also be ready to provide emotional support, when necessary. Teachers and school administration should always be notified of a death in the family. At school, the child's academic performance and social behavior can be observed and teachers can provide necessary support or involve specialized help, if needed. Often grieving children may benefit from extra tutoring and a less demanding schedule. Adolescents need to be repeatedly taught to differentiate among thoughts, feelings, and behaviors. Feelings like anger and rage can and should be expressed in words, not in behavior.

Adolescents will fnd it more helpful to discuss their grief, fears, and feelings with peers or an adult outside of the family, "someone who understands". Parents should be advised to support that, as this is normal behavior for this developmental stage. Support groups for adolescents who are grieving the loss of a loved one, a consultation with a school psychologist or grief psychologist, or help from an adult family friend would be helpful in establishing a trusting dialogue and providing support.

Helping Children Grieve

"And when your sorrow is comforted (time soothes all sorrows) you will be content that you have known me. You will always be my friend. You will want to laugh with me. And you will sometimes open your window, so, for that pleasure . . . And your friends will be properly astonished to see you laughing as you look up at the sky! Then you will say to them, 'Yes, the stars always make me laugh!' And they will think you are crazy. It will be a very shabby trick that I shall have played on you..."

— Antoine de Saint-Exupéry, *The Little Prince* (1900-1944)

Helping children grieve involves understanding their developmental stages and the associated perception of death, loss, and grief at each stage that we discussed earlier. However, there are also general issues applicable to a child of any age going through loss and grief. Grief is a universal feeling and an integral part of life. The child learns how to grieve by looking at parents, other family members, or significant adults in life. The way the child grieves the first loss and the coping mechanism and skills they learn while living through that loss will remain with them for life. This is why it is important to give them your best attention and create an environment where open and honest communication encourages the child to share his or her feelings of sadness, anger, loneliness, and guilt. Grief cannot be resolved without going through pain, but the healing that follows will determine how the child copes with future losses in his/her life.

Feelings

A younger child may not be able to express his or her thoughts and feelings in words. You can acknowledge that you understand the child's sadness by offering a lot of touching, holding, and cuddling. Body contact provides a feeling of security and calms a child. It is normal for a child to cry. Do not rush to get the tears to stop. Crying serves the purpose of releasing the tension of pain.

Older children who can express their thoughts and feelings can be encouraged to share and discuss them if you, as an adult, come forward and share your thoughts and feelings about the loss with the child first. That way you can serve as an example, and it will be easier for the child to open up. If a child acts out angrily, think of an activity that could release the anger and do it together: for example, rip newspapers and magazines, punch pillows, or run outside.

Listen to fears

Much like feelings, fears both rational and irrational need to be acknowledged and not ignored. Attempt to look at the fear from the position of the child and take into consideration the developmental stage of the child.

A child is happy to accept an explanation that will resolve his fears: however, only if it is an explanation that is clear and simple to understand. Brushing off the fear will not help it go away. Hold the child, hug, or touch often while talking about this fear. Tell a story about your own fear or fears and how you learned to cope with them, or a story about someone you and the child know.

Questions about death

As with feelings and fears, questions about death are best answered with honest, clear, and understandable explanations. Use caution when providing explanations, though. Many adults believe it is best to protect the child from harsh realities. Protective statements may haunt the child for a long time. For example, if you say: "When someone dies, it is as if they go to sleep", the child may believe that he or she may die when they go to sleep. If you say: "Your mother has gone to a faraway place", the child may feel abandoned, expect a loved one's return, or instead wish to die as well in order to join the loved one in a faraway place. Help the child understand that death is a natural event that happens to all the living beings at some point of their life. Explain that physical death, as such, does not hurt. The family is sad and crying because they feel the pain of their loss inside, and because they miss the person and the relationship they had with him/her. To help the child avoid being in denial, repeat often that people do not come back when they die; however, the memory of the loved one continues to live in our minds and hearts. Also assure the child that their loved one didn't choose to die and abandon them. Deaths happen due to old age, serious illnesses, accidents, or bad choices that some people make to use alcohol or drugs and then drive. It is not the child's, loved one's, or family's fault.

Provide additional information about the loss as the child matures

Reaching new developmental stages will re-open the grief wound and cause the child to reprocess the experience and the knowledge available about the loss, so far. Encourage open communication so the child can feel free to ask questions about the deceased, circumstances of death, and the meanings of life and death. New grief cycles may then follow, where a child will feel sad, angry, guilty, or face his/her fears again until new coping and healing are achieved.

The power of play

Children express themselves and their thoughts, feelings, and fears through play. Take time to play together outside, or sit down to play inside. Let the child direct the game and lay out the scenario you will follow. The child will then guide the play and express whatever they want through the use of toys and game rules. Toys may feel sad, angry, hit other toys, or be too upset to do anything. Talk through the toys' actions, confirming in words that it is ok to feel what they feel. It is an important assurance to the child that grief causes such feelings.

Events and milestones

Children will mostly miss the deceased at the time of an important event (receiving a prize, a school performance, or a football game) or upon reaching a certain milestone (a birthday or the start or end of primary or secondary school). At holidays, remember the deceased loved one, as this is the time the child will particularly miss him/her. Keeping traditions that were put in place with the deceased person will maintain a sense of stability in the child's life. There may be activities that the child could only do with the deceased (camping with Dad, baking with Mom, or fishing with Grandfather). Often the child will focus on an inability to participate in these particular activities, and it may seem to cause more sadness than the actual death and absence of the person. This is the way a child expresses the pain of loss. Do not criticize the child for missing the activity and not the person: show sympathy and support - that's all the child needs at this time.

Grief in the family

Children can be very sensitive to how other remaining significant people in their lives cope with grief. The emotional collapse of a significant adult is a very difficult situation for the child to handle, and it may cause severe anxiety and insecurity. Try to protect a child from witnessing an emotional collapse of the individuals that the child depends upon. It is enough to gently lead a child out of the room and watch TV together in another room, or play outside. However, sending children away to stay with someone else while the family goes through grief may not be helpful. Children should not be spared from witnessing the reality of what is happening. It is an important lesson to learn, and one that will show them that, despite the great pain, life continues and people can heal and carry on. Being a part of the family means sharing the joy and the sorrow, the happiness and the pain.

Memorial service and funeral

Children need to be included and should be allowed to attend the memorial service and the funeral, if they wish to do that. This brings them in touch with reality and confirms that the death has occurred, thus preventing any ongoing magical wishful thinking that the deceased loved one will return. Acknowledging the loss is an important step in the healing process. If the funeral has passed and the child was not allowed to participate, there are still ways to correct this. A new memorial service can be conducted (different religions have rules for memorial services that can be conducted after the burial) or a short ceremony can be done at the grave site to remember the deceased. The child can bring flowers, photographs, or a gift or a letter to help share his or her feelings.

Ways to remember a loved one

Going to the cemetery helps the child heal from the pain of loss. It helps fight the denial of loss and encourages the release of feelings. A child will actively participate in activities that allow him/her to express love for the deceased one. Helping with the choice of flowers, making a card (or any gift), or writing a goodbye letter are good activities to involve the child in. The gifts and/or the letter or the card can be placed on the grave together with flowers, or buried. If the child wants to keep any photographs or personal items of the deceased, this should be encouraged. Frequent conversations about the deceased loved one will also assure the child of the preservation of memory and a loved one's continuous presence in his/her life.

Involve others

Make sure to notify the kindergarten, school, and all other adults in the child's life of the loss in the family. The child needs to be monitored and supported by people who understand that he or she may be feeling sad, angry, lonely, or might refuse to play or study. Special attention and understanding will help the child cope with tragedy and move on. Learning to cope with losses in life is one of the most important lessons in the child's life; one that will teach coping skills that will be used throughout adulthood.

CHAPTER SIX

Types of Losses

"The reality is that you will grieve forever. You will not 'get over' the loss of a loved one; you will learn to live with it. You will heal and you will rebuild yourself around the loss you have suffered. You will be whole again but you will never be the same. Nor should you be the same nor would you want to."
— Elisabeth Kübler-Ross (1926-2004)

Some losses may be easier to come to terms with than others: for example, the death of elderly family members. Other losses, such as losses of children or young adults to accidents, illnesses, or wars, are far harder to process. When an elderly person dies, I often hear people saying that "he or she lived a good and long life". That doesn't mean that the spouse or the children will not grieve their loss. Every death takes away a part of the life of the grieving person, as well as reminding them about their own mortality and awakening the fear of death.

In general, the death of a child and the death of an elderly person have a lot of similarities and differences as far as the grief process and adapting to the loss are concerned. Due to the nature of the loss and the expectation that parents are expected to die before their children, the loss of a child is an unexpected event; while the loss of an elderly person, in contrast, is usually an expected one. This, however, does not mean that the loss of an elderly person will not evoke emotional distress and grief. The disruption of the child-parent bond causes emotional upset and bereavement irrespective of timing, when it dissolves.

In this chapter we will look at the differences that the loss of a spouse, parent, child, or sibling bring with them. No loss is easy, so by no means should one consider that it may be easier to cope with one type of loss over the other. As we discussed before, our grief depends on the level of attachment and on the type of the relationship we had with the deceased. So the more you cared for the person while he or she were alive and the more you felt attached to and depended upon the person, the more you will grieve the loss of the attachment bond and the more difficult learning to live with that loss will be. This chapter will also talk about the loss of a loved one through suicide.

Anger, despair, emptiness, and being haunted by question "why?" are some of the difficult feelings the loved ones of the deceased go through as they cope with their sudden loss.

Loss of a Parent

"Parting is all we know of heaven and all we
need of hell."
- Emily Dickinson (1830-1886)

For a child, the death of a parent is always a traumatic experience. When the parent of a young child dies, the trauma may lead to long-term psychological harm. Other adults in the life of a child are usually preoccupied with their own grief and often can't provide timely and necessary support to a child, try to fence the child off to protect him from church services, funerals, etc. However, saying last good-byes and having a clear understanding of what happens when a person dies is critical for to child's recovery from grief and adaptation to a parent's death.

The death of a parent when a child is young does not only lead to negative outcomes. There can be positive outcomes too. Children who have lost parents at a young age may possess increased maturity, better coping skills, and be better able to communicate their feelings. They also place higher values on their relationships with other people than those who have not experienced a loss in their early lives.

The death of an elderly person is an expected, nature-driven event. Advancing age is associated with the development of many chronic conditions and an overall decline of biological and immune functions. Adult children can psychologically prepare themselves for the possible death of their elderly parents and, in most cases, are able to come to terms with the loss when it occurs. It is considered to be a normal life course event. Anticipation of the death of an elderly person, however, does not lessen the grief response, because children grow up with the feeling that parents are invincible. The death of a parent is also a major life transition that may spark an evaluation of one's own life and the sense of one's own mortality. Thus, though expected to cope with the death of a parent in a milder, less emotional way, adults may be faced with extremely powerful emotions.

The loss may seem particularly unbearable if the death of a parent occurs at an important or difficult time in the life of the adult during times of emotional stress such, as becoming a parent, divorce, changing jobs or other life-altering milestones. Circumstances of death are also known to impact the grief and bereavement process. Heavy caregiving by the child often brings stronger ties to the parent and greater emotional distress upon death. The location of the death (home, nursing home, distant living) may hold differing impacts on the emotional distress of a surviving child.

Ones relationship with a parent is the longest relationship in the person's life, and the loss of a parent often requires additional strength to be processed. Many people mention the need to be isolated to reconstruct their memories and the details of their relationship with their parent, and they may want to shut out friends and other family members to have more time alone to deal with their pain.

It is important to recognize that the loss of a parent is a profound loss that will cause severe distress, sadness and feelings of loneliness and numbness. It is often said, "as long as your parents are alive, you remain a child". With the death of a parent, childhood is officially "over" and you become next in line on the journey of life. Recognition of loss and acceptance of grief will help ease the pain and maintain ties to the deceased, giving meaning to the loss and emphasizing the continuation of life.

Maria - A Motherless Daughter

"There is something about losing your mother
that is permanent and inexpressable - a
wound that will never quite heal"
~ Susan Wiggs (1958–present)

Maria, a 32-year-old doctoral student, lost her 44-year-old mother when she was 13 years old. Her mother died 6 months after receiving a diagnosis of ovarian cancer. The tumor was diagnosed at a late stage: it had already metastasized to the liver, intestine, and lungs, and there was no possibility of any treatment. All the doctors could offer was end-of-life pain control.

Maria didn't know about her mother's diagnosis until the final weeks of her mother's life, when her mother became too weak to get out of bed. She still remembers crying every day at her mother's bedside, hugging her, and smelling her hair while her mother told her "I love you, I love you, I love you". Maria's father was heartbroken. He could not stop sobbing and seemed to have completely lost the will to live.

After the funeral was over and the hundreds of relatives and friends who came to say their good-byes left, Maria remembers feeling drained and empty. There were no more tears and no energy for crying or even talking. There was nothing to keep her connected to her friends — they all had their mothers next to them, and nobody understood what it felt like to lay your mother to rest and return to an empty house where Mum was no more...

Every item in the house and every little detail had been touched by her mother's hands. It was both a blessing and a curse to be where she once had been. Maria's life changed abruptly and forever.

Maria's father never remarried. Being there for his daughter and supporting her became his reason for living. Despite his help, replacing a mother was not in his power, and Maria felt her absence acutely, more and more every day. Her anger towards her father (for not saving her mother and for not doing enough to prevent her illness) grew. "Why did it have to happen to my mother?", "Why did God have to take my mother and not my father?", "Why couldn't my dad save mom?", and "Why us, why me?" were Maria's thoughts.

Being a teenager at the time of her mother's death, Maria had many questions that were left unanswered. There was nobody to ask about the changes happening to her body or about making the right choices and decisions in her relationships and friendships. Buying a dress for prom was a particularly sentimental moment. Maria felt deprived of her mother's advice and help, and was unsure of herself. This insecurity about her decisions grew stronger. Every choice Maria had to make — choices of university and degree programs, choices of accommodations (dorm or rental apartment), whether to work part-time or concentrate on studying, whether or not to date that gorgeous young man or go out with other girls — "Everything would have been easier if mom was around," thought Maria.

Later on in life, Maria's wedding was both a happy and a distressing event. Maria profoundly felt the absence of her mother. She knew her mother would have wanted to be there to choose the wedding dress and help Maria prepare for the wedding. Maria would have wanted her mother to see how happy she was with her husband. Maria continued to blame everyone and everything for her mother's absence.

Needless to say, every major life event reignited Maria's grief, reminding her again and again of what a huge loss she had suffered upon losing her mother. A motherless child forever: that's how Maria thought of herself. At times Maria felt that her sadness was overwhelming and was hijacking even her happiest moments. Maria's pregnancy and the birth of her twins (a boy and a girl) brought many tears of joy, along with the regret that her mother wasn't there to see them. The twin girl looked like her late grandmother, and every year that similarity seemed to increase: Maria felt she could even recognize some of her mother's moves and facial expressions in her daughter.

"My kids will never know their grandmother. They will never be able to have a relationship with their granny," thought Maria.

Because she was successful in her life and in her career as a public health worker, the agency where Maria worked encouraged her to go for a Ph.D. Maria would become the first in her family to complete a Ph.D. degree. Recognition of this achievement became difficult for Maria to process. Grief and sadness set in again, to the point that Maria felt unable to handle all of her commitments. She knew her mother would have been very proud of her and would have supported her success and stood by her side through the difficult times, but knowing that the most important person in her life would never know about her achievements was eliminating all Maria's much-deserved joy and satisfaction.

She came in to see me initially to get advice on how to cope with family commitments and doctoral program requirements, complaining of being overwhelmed and unable to set priorities. As we began looking into what weights she could assign each of her responsibilities, we stumbled upon her unprocessed grief over the loss of her mother.

It was shocking for Maria to discover that the reason she had trouble managing her life, career, and educational workload was the unprocessed loss of her mother, years and years ago. The truth is that losses of important figures in our lives (in this case, the loss of a mother in Maria's adolescent years) can never be over and done with. The loss co-exists within the bereaved person and accompanies the bereaved throughout his or her life. It is not a linear journey that goes from A (the time of loss) to B (the time when the grief resolves); but, rather, a cycle in which the loss is re-experienced with new strength at every major moment in the grieving person's life. Such loss needs to be integrated into life to allow the bereaved person to move on.

Cognitive therapy helped Maria restructure her understanding of her mother's illness and death and accept that it was neither anyone's fault nor in anyone's power to change the course of events. She also acknowledged that despite her mother's death, her father and other relatives had ensured that she benefitted from their love and affection, was supported in her education, and knew she always had family to count on in difficult situations. Maria identified her feelings of anger and resentment towards her father as unfounded and was brave enough to acknowledge this; first in our sessions and later on in a very important conversation with her dad. This conversation and emotional disclosure between Maria and her father helped Maria's father to also share many of his suppressed emotions. He confessed that Maria's anger towards him made him feel unworthy of being a good dad and unworthy of the promises he'd made to his dying wife to take good care of Maria.

The reconciliation between Maria and her dad, her appreciation of her dad's strong role in her life, and her newfound understanding of all the sacrifices her dad had made to support Maria became the central point of her recovery.

Later we worked on shifting Maria's grief from guilt and sadness into celebrating her mother's life and achievements.

"What would you say was your mother's greatest achievement in life?" I asked Maria.

I still remember how, without hesitation, Maria replied: "It must have been me. She would have been so proud of who I became."

We talked about which of Maria's achievements in life she could dedicate to her mother. The dedication of Maria's dissertation to her late mother gave her a sense of completing something major in her mother's memory. For the first time since her mother's death, Maria felt good about a major milestone in her life.

After completing her dissertation, Maria felt empowered to set up a charity to promote ovarian cancer prevention and research. The charity was set up in the name of Maria's mother and allowed Maria to share her touching story with many women. Maria felt that encouraging women to screen for ovarian cancer helped keep the memory of her mother alive.

Lisa - What I Want My Kids to Know

"If you suppress grief too much, it can well
redouble."

~ Moliere (1622–1673)

Lisa, a 40-year-old executive, lost her 65-year-old father Don to lung cancer. Don was a lawyer. All of his life he led a very healthy lifestyle. He exercised, had been vegetarian for years, made himself fresh juices every morning before work, and would go on detox diets every so often. Yearly check-ups were his thing, too. And if you were wondering by now: no, he never smoked.

Don and his wife took a vacation twice a year. It was on one of the vacations that Don noticed that he became short of breath every time he had to climb the stairs (or, more specifically, his wife noticed). When they got home, Lisa's mother told Lisa that something was not right with Dad. Lisa came over and convinced Dad to go for an extended check-up. She had good connections at the University clinic, where they scheduled a check-up within a couple of days. The x-ray showed a tumor covering most of the right lung. Further tests revealed that the cancer was in an advanced stage. No doctor could explain how such a big tumor could develop despite a recent check-up less than a year ago. Surgery was out of the question. Lisa met up with the best pulmonologist in town, who confirmed that chemotherapy at this late stage would only shorten Don's life. They did want to try some new type of immunotherapy treatment.

In the meantime, Don was getting weaker by the day. He didn't know about his diagnosis, as Lisa had asked the doctors not to tell him about his terminal illness and could not find the strength to break the news to him. Lisa's mother was a strong woman, capable of hiding her worry and anticipatory grief very well. She also thought that it was best not to tell her husband he was dying. The two women united to keep their secret. The story they told to Don was that the pneumonia he had had when he was a teenager had left a shadow and many scars in his lungs. Those scars were acting up now, and there was an inflammation on the site; however, with the right treatment, all the symptoms (weakness, shortness of breath, and dizziness) would soon pass. Don seemed to be happy to live with this illusion. Lisa said: "I felt that he knew things were not good, but he appreciated us not confirming it to him and giving him a chance to live in bliss."

"Why did you decide to not tell your dad about his diagnosis?" I asked.

"I don't know... First, I thought the diagnosis could all be a mistake that would be resolved soon, and so I didn't want to upset Dad with it for no reason. And then, in our culture (Lisa's parents were both of Russian decent), a diagnosis is often hidden from the patient, to protect them from bad news. I have regretted not telling him ever since, though... I wish I could turn back time and tell him."

Very often, especially in cases of a terminal illness diagnosis, relatives face substantial barriers when discussing illness and impending death with the patient. In fact, death and dying are the most difficult issues to discuss for both the terminal patient and their loved ones. When working with families, I often observe how patients and their loved ones enter into a so-called "mutual protective buffering communication" to avoid discussing fears and death-related issues, in an effort to protect each other.

Immunotherapy was presented as a treatment for the old pneumonia scars. The course was completed and the treatment gave Don and his family another year of active, vibrant life. It even allowed Don and his wife to enjoy another beach holiday. He loved the sea so much.

On the way back from his last vacation, Don started coughing up blood. As soon as they came back, they went to see the pulmonologist, who confirmed the worst: the tumor had grown, pushed its way through the airways and blood vessels, and Don's condition would deteriorate from then on. Don was admitted to the hospital to monitor his breathing. He was still not told about his condition. Lisa invented a new lie to keep him comfortable: there was new inflammation on the scar sites in the lungs, but doctors were "promising a quick recovery".

The quick recovery, obviously, never came. Within a week, Don was too weak to even take 20 steps within his room. He lost a lot of weight and his frail body was suffocating from the lack of oxygen. Lisa spent many hours with her father, tortured by the need to maintain the lies she had invented and unable to ask for his last wishes or say her last good-byes.

One morning, a call came in from the hospital. The nurse said: "Your father's condition is not good; he's slipped into a coma. You need to come in as soon as you can." Lisa rushed to the hospital with her mother. They watched Don's breaths become shallower and his face turn grey. He never returned to consciousness and he passed away after his breathing became slower and harsher.

Lisa still remembers the moments when her dad stopped breathing and the horrible realization that she would never be able to talk to him again, to ask for his last wishes or to say goodbye. She would have wanted to tell him how much she loved him, and how everything in her life made sense because he was there.

Lisa's dad had always been a huge support to her. She was his only daughter; the apple of his eye, as they say. He protected her and stood by her in the most difficult moments of her life.

Lisa got pregnant when she was 19. Her boyfriend at the time was not prepared to start a family with Lisa and suggested she go for an abortion. Lisa decided to keep the baby. Lisa's parents stood by her side and supported her decision. Her dad hugged her and said: "Sweetheart, life is the most precious gift you can give. Your mother and I were only fortunate to give one gift, and that was to you. We always wanted more children, but God didn't bless us with any more. Don't think twice: we will help you. That bastard will regret his choice to leave you, one day: trust me."

Despite her parents' assurances, Lisa felt betrayed and heartbroken. Her boyfriend cut off all communication and disappeared from her life completely. Lisa's baby boy, Josh, was born prematurely at 7 months. He was so tiny that everyone was afraid to hold him - except for Lisa's dad. Don embraced this boy from day one as his own son. He spent sleepless nights holding him and rocking him to sleep and then got up in the morning and went to work. Josh grew and putt on the necessary weight in the loving atmosphere of his grandparents' house. Lisa started recovering, as well. She felt grateful for having such wonderful parents, and joy and hope for a new beginning were coming back into her life.

Throughout the turbulent years of coping with being a single mum, finishing her business degree, starting work, and finally settling down with her current husband, Lisa's dad was a constant in her life. Through good and bad times, he was always there, taking care of Lisa and her son. Lisa often thought that had it not be for her parents, she would have never been able to go through that difficult period of her life.

The loss of her dad brought back the feelings of helplessness that Lisa experienced as a young woman when she found out she was pregnant and single. The fear of going through life without her dad's support and his endless ability to listen to her woes and troubles made the anxiety impossible to cope with. Despite being happily married, and having another child with her husband, Lisa now understood her father was by far the most significant relationship of her life.

"Losing him felt like losing a big part of myself: the memories we shared, the tears and heartbreaks he soothed, his hugs that made me feel so safe... I felt I was bleeding inside just thinking of not being able to save him from death."

"What about your mother, Lisa? How was she dealing with her loss?"

"My mom was a strong woman. She did not like to live by her emotions, but always with clear and cold reason. As a young girl, my mother always reminded me of the Snow Queen from the famous tale by Hans Christiaan Andersen. Wise, calculating, and not affected by any storm - my mother could never understand the warm connection I shared with my father. Maybe she was even jealous of us having so much fun. But my mother would never show if anything made her upset or happy."

"When Dad got ill, she was preoccupied with their finances and how she would live now that Dad was not able to work any longer. She was used to a very good life with my father... It took her a long time to rearrange all fund contributions, pensions, and investments, She needed to make sure she would be able to live a decent life after Dad was gone."

"I wondered how she could think about all that at the time when Dad was fighting for his life, but that was just like my mother: calculating and non-emotional. I am not saying she didn't love my father, no. I think she did, but in her own way. They were together and married for 40 years. The life that they lived was engineered by my mother (the social circle of friends they belonged to and the trips they took) and financially supported by my father. It was a mutually beneficial union."

"My mother cried at the funeral - it was probably one of the few times she cried in her life. Right after the funeral, her usual non-emotional side took over. My mom got busy rearranging financials and selling assets she no longer needed (Dad's cars, their summer house). I didn't want to deal with that and was even grateful my mother took over all of these arrangements. She transferred my share of the sale into my bank account, was meticulous about all details, and informed me when all affairs were sorted out and all assets remaining in her possession were duly assigned to me and my children through her will."

"What happened then, Lisa?"

"And then, my mother died. It was a sudden heart attack. She was alone at home. We found her two days later. She had been going through Dad's letters to her, and one of the letters was still in her hand. She was only 61."

Lisa's mother's closed and introverted personality, her inability to share emotional pain and her need to process all feelings and emotions without social support are the most frequent causes of cardio vascular disease. Very often heart attacks happen when a person is unable to share their pain with others. The inability to grieve publicly and openly, non-adequate connections with her daughter and grandchildren, and the lack of social support from those around her had "broken" the heart of that strong woman.

"I would never expect that my mother would die from a heart attack. She seemed invincible throughout the many troubles life served her. But I now think I barely knew my mother and what exactly she felt, as she always had so much trouble sharing her feelings."

In Lisa's therapy we focused on the two different grief experiences that the deaths of Lisa's mum and dad had brought about. With Lisa's dad, it was the guilt of not being able to protect him and the fear of living life without him. With Lisa's mum, initially it was guilt over never taking time to understand and get to know her. As Lisa said: "Mum was always so self-sufficient, so strong…" Later on in therapy, we discovered Lisa's insecurity and fear of being able to live her life without her mother. Only after her mother's death did Lisa understand how much her mother took care of her, even though she never displayed it publicly, and how sound all of her financials and investments were. Lisa confessed she never told her mother how much she loved her, and was sorry that she would never have the chance to do that. It lead Lisa to re-evaluate the relationships she had with her husband and children. She learned from the sudden death of her mother that it is important to tell loved ones how much you care for them every day, and to hug and kiss them whenever there is a chance. "I hope I have a long life ahead of me, but if I were to die of a heart attack tomorrow, I would want my kids to know how much I love them."

Jane - A Humiliation of Alzheimer's Disease

"There can be no hope without fear, and no
fear without hope."
— Baruch Spinoza (1632-1677)

Jane, a 59-year-old art historian, struggled to come to terms with the death of her mother Helen, who passed away after a long and painful progression of Alzheimer's disease. Jane understood that her 80-year-old mother's decline and death were expected; but she still suffered from enormous guilt. When asked to specify what, exactly, she felt guilty about, Jane suggested that it would be necessary to take a look at her late mother's life.

Her mother was a renowned art expert who, during the course of her career, was involved in consulting with major museums, art galleries, and private collectors, and who appraised art objects in the area of her expertise. A fine and classy woman, she projected an image of finesse and sophistication and exhibited an almost bibliographical memory of her subject and the overall history of art. Her aristocratic manners won her sympathy and cemented her reputation in all circles and in the society events she so loved to attend.

As a child, Jane remembers living in awe of her mother; adoring her every appearance, gesture, and word. Jane also said she always feared not being able to live up to her mother's high standards. Her mother was the ideal of everything Jane ever wanted to achieve.

Years passed. Jane's father died and Helen was 68 when she became a widow. Jane lived in the same city with her husband and two children. Jane's life and career were still vastly influenced by her mother - or, more correctly, by her mother's expectations of her. About ten years into her widowhood, although still very active in her work, Helen started to display the first symptoms of what later would be diagnosed as Alzheimer's disease. It started with losing keys, forgetting appointments, and confusing dates – nothing serious enough to have caught Jane's attention - until one day she got a phone call from her mother's neighbor, who was alarmed by the smell of smoke coming from the apartment. Jane rushed to her mother's house, arriving shortly after firefighters broke into the apartment and found Helen sleeping in her bed. It turned out that Helen had forgotten she was cooking soup on the kitchen stove, and had gone to bed. The burned soup leftovers in the pot had caused the smoke, and the timely reaction of the neighbors had saved Helen's apartment and life. While helping her mother air the apartment and clean the kitchen cabinets, floors, and surfaces which had turned black from smoke, Jane discovered multiple packages containing money. Various amounts of cash were stashed in pots, rice and bean containers, vases, knife compartments, and even in a detergent box under the sink. When Jane asked her mother if she remembered any other places where cash could be hidden, her mother would only say she didn't think the money belonged to her, or that she didn't have anything to do with hiding it.

Jane finally began suspecting that there was a memory problem going on. She promptly organized a consultation with a neurologist and convinced her mother to undergo a check-up. The diagnosis crushed any hope Jane had that this could be a temporary impairment. The doctor suggested that Alzheimer's disease was advancing to Stage 2, and Jane had to make some drastic decisions about her mother's care, as the decline could occur at a faster pace from then on.

Alzheimer's disease (AD) is a progressive neurodegenerative disorder of the central nervous system that leads to the most common form of age-associated dementia. The first clinical symptoms of AD include a loss of recent memory, faulty judgment, personality changes, and a progressive loss of reasoning power. Intermediate stages are marked by confusion, irritability, anxiety, and speech deterioration. Later stages of AD lead to patient's agitation, aggressiveness, and delusional conditions. With sleep disturbances accompanied by a loss of reasoning, the patient deteriorates to the point that even simple responses such as swallowing and controlling the bladder are difficult. AD patients experience difficulty labeling emotions as sadness, anger, fear, or surprise. About 10% of the general population over the age of 65 suffers from the disease, and the proportion is about 35% in those over 85.

Jane made arrangements to have her mother move in with her. A guest room with an enclosed bathroom was used to accommodate Helen until other care decisions could be made. At first Helen was still involved in family life, present at the dining table during family meal times and able to maintain a conversation. Although she asked many questions repeatedly, she was still able to follow the answers. However, that didn't last long. Her personality started changing abruptly. From an elegant and polite woman, Helen was turning into a different person. Bitter, angry, violent at times, even swearing – this was opposite of the always-elegant and refined woman and mother whom Jane adored and remembered.

One morning Jane came into her mother's room in the morning to find her sitting on the floor, mumbling something to herself. When Jane kneeled down to come closer and hear what she was saying, her mother looked up, grabbed her by her hair, and started shouting "Hold her, hold her, this is the woman who stole my diamonds! Help, help, she is a thief!!!"

Jane's husband, housemaid, and children all ran in to find Jane fighting to free herself from the hands of her mother, who was pulling her down by her hair, punching her with her legs, and swearing. The doctor was called for consultation.

He was sorry events were taking such a rapid turn for the worse and prescribed more medication; mostly to calm Helen. The doctor also suggested that the family should get extra help by moving Helen to a nursing facility. Jane declined and said she could not allow her much respected and elegant mother to be seen in such humiliation and degradation by anyone but her own family. Jane's husband withdrew into his work: he spent longer hours in the office, scheduled more trips to conferences and seminars, and, when at home, asked not to be disturbed when the doors of his home office were closed, which became a constant state.

Jane was left alone to handle her caregiving duties. Luckily, she could still have help from the housemaid, who came in every day and would sometimes stay the night. Jane felt utterly exhausted by her mother's night wanderings and violent outbreaks. Every day, Jane had to witness the humiliating degradation of her ideal mother into a stranger she neither recognized nor wished to know. She found herself growing increasingly angry, agitated, and often angry with this stranger, who by now had stopped recognizing her as her daughter. She could see no sign of clarity in her mother's eyes: it often seemed like some demonic being had taken over the body of her poor mother and was controlling her speech and behavior. There were no good days with all of this swearing, punching, and aggression; and then incontinence and a complete loss of stool control set in. Jane had to stop working as she became a full-time nurse and cleaner. Stress was building up, and there were times when Jane could not control herself any more, giving way to crying and venting, often in an abusive manner towards her mother. Jane cried again when she remembered the times when she could not control herself and punched her mother back, or held her down more forcefully than she should have. There was nothing left to respect in this troubled relationship. "It was like the evil had set out to destroy my mother and any loving memory I had of her," said Jane.

Months of agony that seemed to last forever came to an abrupt end when Helen suffered aspirational pneumonia, the most common cause of death in Alzheimer's disease. Aspirational pneumonia happens when the patient loses control of the swallowing function and aspirates pieces of food while eating, or small quantities of fluid while drinking. This leads to the inflammation of airways, bronchus, and lungs.

The end of Helen's life came very quickly. Jane says that in her final hours, her mother seemed to have found her serenity. As she neared the end of her life, she held her daughter's hand and stroked her fingers. It almost felt like her soft and delicate personality had returned; if not to say a final good-bye, then to indicate it by a tender touch of fingers. Those final hours brought Jane to the realization that it was her mother who was dying and it had always been her mother, even in the most degrading moments of her final years and in the aggressive outbursts that marred the memories Jane held of her. The guilt of not controlling herself around the ill and weak individual that her mother became turned Jane's life into a never-ending nightmare. How could she lose her temper when her mother was dealing with the loss of her memory, personality, and dignity? Jane could not forgive herself and could find no justification for the irritability and anger that took over most of the times she cared for her mother. Grief became a constant reminder of how wrongly and cruelly she had treated her mother.

Looking back, she felt she was never able to tell her mother how much she loved and adored her, how much her elegance and knowledge motivated Jane to excel in life, and how sorry she was that her mother had to go through such a degrading condition as Alzheimer's disease, a condition that robbed herself and her mother of a meaningful relationship in the last years of Helen's life.

In meetings with Jane, we discussed the reasons why irritability was normal under the circumstances of the intense, life-changing caregiving duties Jane had had to undertake full-time to look after her ill mother. Caregiving is known to have serious detrimental effects on the mental and physical health of caregivers. Many caregivers face severe psychological distress. Anticipation of negative outcomes, anticipatory grief, emotional distress from watching their loved ones suffer from pain, weakness, and deterioration, an inability to change the course of events, feelings of guilt, resentment, and disappointment: all have a profound impact on caregivers' mental health.

Often caregivers also need to deal with verbal and physical aggression, confusion, and anger which may accompany some dementia and terminal cancer conditions, as was the case with Helen's condition. Many caregivers of patients with Alzheimer's disease blame the condition for robbing their loved ones of memory, dignity, personality, and respect. Coping with such intense emotional stressors and anticipatory grief becomes a necessary adjustment in the lives of a patient's family members.

Feelings of guilt and self-reproach after prolonged caregiving are also common and major emotional stressors that need to be dealt with in order to achieve resolution. Jane has benefitted from understanding that her feelings of resentment and anger towards her ill mother had nothing to do with her mother: they were the sign of emotional stress, fatigue, and anticipatory grief over the physical and mental decline of her mother's condition and the realization of her approaching loss. Gradually, over the course of several months of cognitive therapy, Jane made peace with herself and was able to find forgiveness in her grief.

Loss of a Spouse

"There are things that we don't want to happen but have to accept, things we don't want to know but have to learn, and people we can't live without but have to let go."

- Author Unknown

The death of a spouse, whether at young or an older age, is usually a very profound loss. Spouses share between them their lives, interests, memories, social contacts and relationships with relatives, children and friends; thus, losing a spouse is often described by widows and widowers as losing a "half" of themselves. Learning to live alone without a lifetime partner is a much harder adjustment than one can imagine. After many years of marriage, habits are difficult to change, starting life with a new partner is unlikely; and in a young marriage the loss of a spouse also brings with it the loss of future plans for a life together.

In many cultures it is common for widows to wear black for a period of one or two years to signify their mourning over the loss of their husband, while in some religions and cultures (for example, Greek Orthodox), the widows will continue to wear black for the rest of their lives.

The death of a spouse requires that the surviving spouse makes arrangements for the funeral and organizes the ceremony. If the death was not expected, this task can be emotionally draining. Sorting out financial tasks, making changes to bank accounts and insurance policies, and honoring will arrangements also add pressure to the stress of loss. There is just too much for the grieving person to handle in the first days, weeks, and months.

For most couples, there tasks are divided. For example, the husband may work in the garden or pay the bills, while the wife prepares meals, cleans the house, and does the laundry. The death of a spouse brings not only intense grief over the loss and dissolution of a life bond, but also added responsibilities for the widow/widower. The surviving spouse will almost always face social isolation, as many groups of common friends are couples and it may be difficult for both couples and the bereaved to reconnect when the balance of communication is lost.

There is a difference in the type of grieving experience the widows/widowers may deal with depending on the type of death, on whether it was expected (such as with old age or advanced illness) or unexpected (an act of violence, accident, or sudden illness). In case of an expected death, it may be preceded by anticipatory grief, which we have discussed in the earlier chapter of this book. while in case of an unexpected death, it can be compared to a traumatic shock which is difficult to handle and may often require seeking professional help to cope with the loss and carry on with new life.

The common feelings in grief for widows/widowers are depression, loneliness, helplessness, hopelessness, and emotional instability. There may be need for increased social support, so it is often helpful if one of the close relatives or adult children help with the funeral arrangements, financial transformations, and household changes. Bereaved spouses often report needing extended time to learn to live alone, appreciate life, and find new meaning in the past and future. Processing the loss helps them move forward, find pleasure in life again, and build up hope for the future.

Al - Fighting Cancer

"There's this place in me where your
fingerprints still rest, your kisses still linger
and your whispers softly echo. It's the place
where a part of you will forever be a part of
me."

- Anonymous

Al, a 69-year-old retired executive, lost his 57-year-old wife Linda 2 years ago. A year before she died, Linda was diagnosed with stage 4 pancreatic cancer. She was only 56 and had just become the Dean of the University where she was teaching. At the time she was diagnosed, she was having stomach pains that couldn't be explained, and further testing revealed it was a tumor in her pancreas. The cancer was metastatic: it had already spread to her lungs and her liver. The inevitable reality hit Linda and Al when they were told that she had less than a year to live at best, with little to no treatments available.

Within two months of her diagnosis, Linda was bed-bound, on a feeding tube, and oxygen-dependent. Too weak to receive any therapy, Linda's functional status steadily declined. Many nights Al sobbed as he sat next to her and held her hand. Their life together passed in front of his eyes: Linda in a summer dress at the beach where they met, then on their wedding day, the birth of their son, their new house. Linda's spirit and vitality always gave Al strength; but now her strength was gone and her vitality was slipping away. Linda finally succumbed to her illness and died in her bed at home. Al and their son were next to Linda as she took her last breath.

Al came into therapy a year after Linda's death. His grief was intense. Al complained of not being able to sleep and of having flashbacks of Linda's death.

"Losing Linda was the most painful thing that ever happened to me. I know nobody can ever be prepared for grief. It can't be predicted. But when I think of Linda not being there, not being alive anymore ... I get this overwhelming, sobbing pain. It hurts, but I also know I don't want this pain to go away. This is how Linda is staying with me, and I never want to lose her. My many friends, relatives and ex-colleagues all provide support, but I want to be alone in my grief. I don't want to share the pain of losing Linda."

"The pain of grief is different for everyone. Nobody can share yours even if they wanted to. How is your son coping with his grief?"

"He is much stronger than me. He went back to work the next day after the funeral. He comes to see me every Sunday, and we drink our beers on the porch and talk about his work. He doesn't even mention his mother or say that he misses her."

"But that doesn't mean he is not grieving. Some people hide their feelings and prefer to deal with pain on their own terms. Perhaps he also feels that you need to be distracted from your grief and not be reminded of your loss, and doesn't want to touch the subject of your loss when he sees you."

"Our son took after Linda. She refused to be taken down. No matter what the difficulty or setback, she was always the cheerful one; the one to smile when she felt pain, and the person who encouraged someone when they felt lost, or comforted them when hope was gone."

"Even in her last months of life, when we knew that there were no treatments left and the doctor recommended that Linda be moved to hospice for comforting care and pain control, her spirit never changed. She was weak, debilitated, fragile, and only resembled the person I knew before, but her spirit was as strong as ever. Her spirit was much bigger than the illness that took her life. Do you see what I mean?"

"I do, Al, I really do; and it seems to me you have just found a key to coping with your grief. Linda's illness and death left a lesson for you to learn. The lesson was: no matter how heavy the hardship that hit her, her spirit helped her remain strong and even supported you during that hardship. I imagine that if you acknowledge that, her spirit could continue to support you even after her death."

"Remember her vitality, her spirit, her love for life. Although the illness debilitated her physical body, the essence of her spirit never changed. Linda's death could teach all of us a lesson on how to live and be happy, no matter what. Being grief-stricken is like being ill, and the ability to see beyond the pain and to allow an aching heart to open up and share this pain could help your spirit to emerge and carry you through these hard times. Coping with grief doesn't mean forgetting the person you have lost. It means incorporating the loss into your life going forward and finding meaning in carrying on in loving memory of Linda, or in being there for your son and his future children. Linda will always be in your heart and will be forever missed."

Al stayed in therapy for several months more, but that conversation was a true turning point on the road to his recovery. Although the pain of his loss still throbbed in Al's heart, he continued to build the strength to live with that loss. In the absence of Linda, he relied on the memory of Linda's spirit to give him strength and support him through the hard times. Al became a grandfather two years after he finished therapy. I was glad to hear that his granddaughter's name was Linda.

Anna - Learning to Live

"He that conceals his grief finds no remedy for
it".
- Turkish Proverb

Anna, a 47-year-old office manager, lost her 52-year-old husband Rob five years ago. Rob was a high-ranking government official, and he died in his sleep of a sudden heart attack. Anna was a housewife at the time of her husband's death. After they got married, she never had to work. Their daughter was born soon after Rob and Anna got married and she was 10 years old when Rob passed away.

Anna's married life was full of positive memories. Her husband provided for her every need, and they lived in a lovely house. Anna occupied herself with household chores and her little daughter and kept busy attending many social and public events with her husband. Her worries included what outfit to buy and wear for the next event or dinner, and where to go for the next vacation.

When Rob passed away so suddenly, Anna was completely unprepared. Rob never talked about what would happen in the event of his death. At 52, Rob was just not planning on dying. And yet he was gone, and now Anna had to figure a way to go on living while raising their daughter.

"I felt crushed and abandoned," Anna recalls of her feelings in the first days and weeks after Rob passed away. "To prepare for the funeral, I had to go to the bank and get money to pay for everything. It was the first time I went to check our shared account. There was enough money to pay for the funeral service and perhaps a couple of months of expenses, but there was not enough money to sustain our life if I didn't figure out a way to start working."

In the coming months, Anna was busy taking ownership of the house they lived in (it was registered in her husband's name). There were some papers in his office indicating some investments, but nothing major. Anna had to sell their country house and two of her husband's cars to have enough money for the daily living expenses, but it was clear she needed to find work.

"I had no time to grieve or to sit down and cry. Rob left me so early. Our marriage was never a passionate one: rather, it was a match made in both of our interests. My family wanted me to marry a man with a stable future, and Rob needed a young and appropriate wife to support him in his political career. But I did grow to love him over the years. Losing him was a blow I didn't expect, and I don't think I realized how much our daughter was suffering the loss of her father. She was only ten and I didn't know how to talk to her about death. When Rob died, I hardly knew what to do. It was the first time I saw a dead body myself."

"So what did you say to your daughter?"

"Initially, I wanted to tell her that her father went on a trip, thinking I would be able to win time and figure out what to tell her; but she walked into our room when I was on the phone to the police. I didn't notice that she was standing by the door and listening to what I was describing. When I hung up, and before the police arrived, I hugged her and told her that Daddy has died and we have to be strong for each other."

"I remember that she grabbed me around my waist and hid her face in my tummy, sobbing and crying. My father and my stepmother arrived just minutes after that and took my daughter with them to keep her out of the house, where police and ambulance arrived to check the body of my husband and take him away."

"When the funeral was over, I remember that my daughter didn't want to go back to school. She clung to me every moment. Maybe she was scared of losing me too."

In the months that followed, Anna had to discover life as she never thought she would have to do. Searches for a job were difficult for someone who had never worked in her life. She did have a good education and a degree in English literature, but no experience working and no idea what she could do to earn a living. Friends suggested looking for a job as an office administrator or an assistant to an executive, and that's what Anna was doing. Many friends that her husband and she were close to disappeared right after Rob's death.

"After I found the position of an office administrator in a consulting office, the lives of my daughter and I changed. I had to make arrangements for someone to be with her in the afternoons after school until I golt home from work at 7 or sometimes 8 o'clock at night. There was hardly time for us to catch up and talk. I felt tired from spending all day in the office and trying to fit into a new world. The salary wasn't great and we had to make adjustments to our expenses. I was trying to make a smooth transition so that my daughter would not notice the change in our lifestyle. We had to stop her tennis lessons, cut down on shopping, and rent out the basement of our house to a tenant. Money was tight, but at least we were providing for ourselves."

Once Anna's life started to stabilize, the pain of grief truly struck her. She couldn't sleep at night for thinking of what would happen to her daughter if she were to die as unexpectedly as Rob. She was terrified about dying. The realization that death could come unexpectedly was a nightmare ("If Rob could die, so could I."). The traumatic experience of losing her husband and the family's sole bread winner, plus the loss of her comfortable, wealthy lifestyle and of many possessions shifted Anna into a state of severe death anxiety.

She entered therapy at that point. Her intense anxiety did not let her sleep at night. The fear of dying suddenly and of leaving her daughter alone was overwhelming. We worked through Anna's fears and the therapy helped her to accept her mortality and to prepare for the worst outcome. However, this also led to a significant personal change. Anna embraced her life as a daily chance to fulfill everything she wanted to do for herself and for her daughter, and to fill her life with as much love, joy, and excitement as she could. "If I die tomorrow, I know my daughter will remember all the love and good times we had together".

Anna's processing of grief led her to discover her fears but also reminded her of the importance of living each day as though it was the last day of her life, of appreciating and loving her loved ones, of spending more time creating memories together, and learning to be more independent and self-confident by taking control of her own life. All these lessons were given to Anna by her grief. The memory of her husband and the father of her daughter gave Anna a gift of life.

Katie - The Story of Us

"All happy families are alike; each unhappy
family is unhappy in its own way."
- Leo Tolstoy, *Anna Karenina* (1828-1910)

Katie, a 46-year-old journalist came into
therapy seeking help for a personal loss. She was
grieving the loss of her husband Ben. Katie and
Ben met at a friend's house twenty years ago.
Katie said it was love at first sight.

"He still is the love of my life; a love that
began so many years ago and brought me so
much happiness and pain."

Three months after they met, Ben proposed,
and Katie thought this was the way it was
supposed to be. It felt natural, right, and
destined.

Katie was only 26 years old. Not ready to
settle down, she was enjoying the free life of
dating and outings for drinks and dinners with a
company of friends. Ben had been married
before. After he caught his wife cheating on him,

he went through a painful separation. It was not as much of a pain to split up from the cheating wife, but it hurt him that he had to give up seeing his little daughter every day. He stayed close to the little one, ensuring her well-being and spending as much time as he could with her during weekends and summer and Christmas holidays.

Katie embraced Ben's life and commitments, moved into his house, and was ready to settle down in her new life. Preparations for the wedding consumed all of her time. She quit her regular job and did only freelance assignments. Ben was happy, and so in love.

Their fairytale wedding took place in the summer. Katie can still remember the exact date, and her happiness on that day. Arriving at the church with Ben and his parents waiting outside was the happiest moment of her life.

"Katie, you say you were separated only 2 years after the wedding. What went wrong?"

"Ben was a jealous kind. I think that the experience from his first marriage made him very suspicious. He was afraid of being cheated on again. He was trying to protect himself from another painful revelation of unfaithfulness. At first, I tried to prove to him that I was to be trusted, that I was faithful. But day after day, it became more and more difficult. It felt like I had "to justify myself for crimes I haven't committed". He wanted to know what I was doing, who I was talking to, where I was going. The total control became overwhelming. Eventually, I started snapping back. I felt I just couldn't live with this lack of trust anymore. It was demeaning."

Katie said that her pride took over, and she packed her stuff and moved out of their house. She didn't cheat on Ben, nor was planning to, and felt offended that she had to convince Ben of her innocence. Ben filed for divorce. Katie spent weeks at her parents' house sobbing into her pillow. As the pain wore off, she rented a small apartment and moved there, found a job, and tried to re-build her life from scratch.

Her new job involved a lot of traveling. It helped ease the pain, but every time she came home, the memories of Ben haunted her. On one of her returns she found a voicemail from Ben asking that they meet and talk. Katie got in the car and drove to their favorite restaurant. They had a few drinks at the bar. Ben said he could not think about anything but his love for her. He could simply not live without her. That night they made up. They still loved each other so much.

Life was perfect. Katie and Ben felt they needed no one else. They didn't want to have kids yet; they wanted to enjoy each other - their mornings before work, dinners, and nights full of passion.

But Katie's work began to interfere with their life. There was still a lot of traveling, late night work, and business dinners to attend. Ben became jealous again. His work wasn't doing well, at the time. He was fighting to keep his business alive. Katie's involvement at work and her excitement about the projects under her supervision caused Ben to feel unworthy.

Ben also knew there were many men around Katie at work. Their attention and natural courtship of Katie, who was a beautiful woman, caused him to feel jealous and left out. Arguments set in. Katie tried to justify herself, but it never helped. Ben was shutting himself off, and their intimacy was falling apart.

Katie still remembers their last trip together. It was Ben's birthday and she decided to surprise him with a week-long trip to one of the beach resorts. The beautiful hotel, relaxing days at the pool, and blissful dinners and nights seemed to help them put all of their differences behind them again. Ben enjoyed unwrapping the birthday gift that Katie had wrapped in 20 boxes, each smaller than the other. They were happy again.

Upon returning from their vacation, Katie was back at work and Ben tried not to show his jealousy but was feeling left out again. No matter how much Katie tried, she knew that Ben's problems at work were taking away their happiness. One day when Katie had to work on a Saturday, she came home and found Ben on the couch in the living room, ready to leave.

He said, "Katie, I have to leave. I can't take this anymore. I love you, but I can't watch you live your life without me. I will miss you terribly, I know. But if I stay, I know I will die of heartache."

Katie begged him to stay: "Please don't walk away. I love you. It's just my work, I need you next to me. Stay, let us have just a little more time together."

Ben walked out and closed the door behind him. He didn't know Katie was pregnant. She had found out the day before and was preparing to tell him.

Two weeks later, Ben still hadn't called. Katie couldn't stand the idea of calling and bringing him back because she was pregnant, so she agreed to have an abortion. She never told him they were expecting a child.

Through common friends, Katie found out that Ben left the country: he had found a job someplace else. Katie recovered from the abortion. Pain and grief over the lost baby were killing her, but she resolved to stay strong.

Three years passed before Katie saw Ben again. They ran into each other at a restaurant. Ben asked if Katie wanted to have a coffee and talk. He talked about his love and how separating from Katie had destroyed his life.

"I was not happy with my life, either. After I split up with Ben, my heart was broken. I saw other men and even had another relationship going on in my life, but it was never the same as it was with Ben."

"Ben said he could give everything for another chance. He said if we had a baby perhaps we could still be together. I couldn't hold myself and started crying. I told him that I was pregnant when he left me three years ago and that I had an abortion and killed our baby."

"When Ben heard that, he got up and walked out without saying a word. I tried to call him, but he said he never wanted to talk to me again because I had killed his child without telling him about it and asking if he wanted us to keep the baby."

"And what happened then? You are grieving that Ben died and you had no chance to talk to him and find peace before he passed away?"

"He never died. He is very much alive. But I died for him. And I grieve my death in his life every day. Can't you grieve a loss of a person who is alive but wants no contact with you because of a mistake you've made?"

"I guess you can, Katie. Grief is a reaction to any form of catastrophic loss in your life. And losing Ben was a tragic event for you."

In the months to come, I worked with Katie on accepting the guilt for hurting Ben, on forgiving him for hurting her, on recognizing that their relationship was turbulent and required a lot of work, on expressing gratitude that he was her husband, and on admitting that he would always be a part of Katie's life as the past can never be erased and forms the present as well as shaping the future.

Grief may come in many different forms and shapes. The loss of a loved one from the break-up of a significant relationship through divorce and separation can resemble the loss of a loved one to death, and requires time and effort to be processed. A divorce is never easy. Mourning for the lost loved one is always there. One never truly gets over it, but the pain eases. Katie's story is a true confirmation of that.

Loss of a Child

"To spare oneself from grief at all cost can be achieved only at the price of total detachment, which excludes the ability to experience happiness."
- Erich Fromm (1900-1980)

As parents, we anticipate our children will survive us, and there are multiple reasons to explain that. Our children carry our legacy and family and cultural history: our genetic blueprint. They hold our dreams, aspirations, and hopes for the future. Their lives confirm our immortality as we live on in and through our children into the grandchildren and beyond. Children give meaning and a sense of purpose to their parents' lives. The grief over a child's death is much more severe than the loss of a spouse, parent, or sibling.

Outliving one's child is unnatural. Human nature is programmed to reproduce and create offspring, thus ensuring the continuity of life and one's immortality. The creation of life requires further efforts to preserve its existence, and this is a task which reflects the biological and symbolic meanings of parenthood. The bond between a parent and a child is strong, necessary for survival, and lasts long after one member of the bond dies.

In parents, a child's loss brings about the disruption of functioning, holding a depressive effect and bringing guilt for not having done enough to save and protect the child. It's a mortal wound: many parents say they feel a part of them was torn away. Parents face difficulty in accepting the loss and finding meaning in the death of a child. Years and decades later, the gap in their lives cannot be replaced with anything, and their relationship with the deceased child may remain highly emotional. Whether the death of the child occurred due to an accident, illness, or violence, the guilt for surviving and for not having protected the child from harm remains strong in a parent and is always a traumatic experience. Grief over the loss of a child may also include miscarriage and stillbirth. Mothers who suffer miscarriage or regret abortions may deal with great hidden emotional pain and may resent other pregnant women.

Parents suffer and seek to answer the question "why" as they go back to the tragic event of their child's death. Diminished self-esteem, despair, and a strong desire to be reunited with their deceased child brings suicidal thoughts to many parents. Many of them report feeling that the only way to end the unbearable pain of a child's loss is to end their life. Risk of suicide is high in parents suffering from the loss of a child.

The family also loses its wholeness. The loss of a child causes major distress not only in parents, but in all family members. Grandparents grieve for the loss of their grandchild but also for the pain that their adult child has to suffer. Surviving siblings may be subject to even more losses: the loss of a sibling as well as the loss of parents who, in their grief, lack energy to function as parents to the surviving child.

When a child becomes terminally ill, other children in the family find themselves "imprisoned" by the illness or the sibling and the sorrow of their parents. Parental attention focuses on the ill child, leaving the healthy siblings behind. This may create feelings of insignificance and a belief that the dying or deceased child is more important to parents. Children witness the toll the illness takes on their parents, and they try hard to help and support. However, being young also means that they are not always kept informed about their ill sibling's condition. Parents are distressed, irritable, often have a tense relationship with each other, and become unable to participate in the life, development, and activities of other children. These children feel neglected, lonely, and lack an understanding of the events, however, and are often unable to express their feelings to their already-distressed parents. Wishing to protect their parents, the other children in the family may hide emotional and physical pain from them. Their relationship with the ill and dying sibling may also be strained, as the mutual give-and-take balance is disrupted and the ill child may wish to buffer contact with the well sibling in an effort to avoid emotional pain from both sides.

The loss of a sibling requires a child to cope with their own grief and adapt to many changes in their home. The normal family life is over, and children have no control of their lives and are deprived of the activities their classmates can enjoy. It often happens that the grief of siblings, particularly those of young ages, is overlooked. Nobody talks to them about the nature of the deceased sibling's illness, circumstances of death, or general questions relating to death and dying. Children feel isolated and neglected. Lack of valid information gives way to distorted imagination, the development of wrong ideas, and many fears about death that may lead to developmental problems and psychological difficulties.

After the loss of a child in the family, the relationships between parents and other surviving children changes. At first, parents may be unable to take care of their other children. And then there may be new parental expectations, over-protectiveness, and a reluctance to discipline or to allow children to engage in normal or risky experiences. Parents may use the surviving children or children born after the death of their child as "replacement children", attributing them with identities of the deceased child and thus neglecting their unique identities and personalities.

Terminal illness and loss of a child have a severe impact on the spousal relationship of a child's parents. In cases where terminal illness precedes the death, parents experience enormous emotional, physical, and financial stress.

Work commitments may not be achievable as parents need more time off work to take care of their dying child. It is often the mother who undertakes the full-time care, while fathers become sole providers of the family in such stressful times. The imbalance of the relationship leads to strain.

Each side may feel underappreciated: the mother for her increased involvement with a sick child and many emotionally and physically distressing duties, and the father for having to work two and sometimes even three jobs to meet financial demands. Fathers may also feel isolated, excluded from the child's care, and thus frustrated. Sexual intimacy is diminished or completely lost due to physical exhaustion and heavy emotional strain during the time of grief. Most couples report that it took a year or two to restore a sexual relationship. The loss of a child shutters the world of each parent and they tend to isolate themselves from each other, searching for ways to cope with the loss. Talking to one another becomes painful and difficult.

There are major differences between genders in ways of coping and grieving. In general, women are able to express their grief more openly. Mothers who lost their child can mourn their loss more intensely and demonstrate their grief in public more openly than can fathers. At the time of loss, fathers feel the need to support their grieving wives who, through tears, express their pain and despair. Not seeing the same emotional reaction from their husbands, mothers feel angry over their husbands' unwillingness to share their grief, tears, and mourning.

Men face difficulties coping with emotional burdens and may resort to passive coping strategies, withdrawal, and denial. Their wives may not be able to understand this and engage in arguments and angry outbursts, demanding increased emotional involvement and support. This only further alienates the couple and may break bonds during this difficult time.

A substantial number of marriages can not survive the loss of a child and end in separation and divorce. This is particularly true for couples with marital problems present before their child's death. However, in the majority of cases, the bond between parents survives the major ordeal and becomes even stronger.

In the initial weeks after the child's death, relatives and friends may play a major support role, helping the parents take care of the remaining children and doing some household chores. Such support is as important as emotional support. The void left by the death of the child can't be filled. Parents who lost their child report feeling like they were in a daze, especially during the first year after the loss, and do not remember how they managed to get through those early days and weeks of their grief.

When a child is lost, parents need to confront the painful aspect of the loss and integrate and transform their grief. Coping with the loss of a child involves a combination of action and cognitive work. Emotional pain kept inside does not disappear and may surface in destructive ways, physically (to the individual) and socially (to the relationships of the individual). Emotional pain may be eased through talking about the loss, and crying.

Dysfunctional thoughts and beliefs need to be restructured. Restructuring dysfunctional thoughts includes confronting false beliefs and expectations and finding a deeper meaning in loss. Many parents find relief by being involved in purposeful activities that prevent them from becoming totally consumed by their grief. This could include a to focus on creating a legacy for the surviving parent and their deceased child through other channels, for example, or working to change, or volunteering to help others with conditions that contributed to their child's death, establishing scholarship fund in their child's name, setting up charity organizations, or helping with charity events.

Reading books about loss and learning about the experiences of others who went through similarly difficult times helps parents deal with their sense of isolation and identify with the feelings of other people. Support groups and online forums for parents who lost their child may also prove helpful, as they provide a safe place for sharing emotional pain, learning coping strategies that helped others, and lend support.

Religion may serve as a major source of comfort and strength in grief for those who are religious, although many parents initially express anger at God for not having protected their child and for having betrayed them. Many parents renew or question their spiritual or religious beliefs. Frequent visits to the cemetery, especially in the initial phases after the loss, help many parents cope and continue communicating with their lost child. Through the loss of a child, parents learn to embrace their own mortality and the beauty of life "here and today", realize the fragility of life, develop a deeper appreciation of life, discover inner strengths, and change their life priorities. Finally, parents become aware of being there for other loved ones (such as other surviving children) who are suffering, especially in cases where a family's loss of a child results in losing both a sibling and the parent who is no longer able to care for them.

The process of healing after the devastating loss of a child is a long one. A bond between a deceased child and a parent continues for the rest of life. The pain of the loss, unfortunately, is just as long. It may diminish at times and then become acute again, triggered by the approach of a special date (a deceased child's birthday or anniversary of death) as well as the big milestones that the child could have achieved (such as the child's friends graduating school or getting married).

Memories of the child may be connected to a playground, to the songs the child used to enjoy listening to or singing, or to favorite toys. Parents learn to live with their pain, and understand that they will never get "over" the death but instead must assimilate and live with it. With this understanding comes hope for the future, while not losing connection with the past and the lost child.

Megan - Frozen in Grief

> "Do not judge the bereaved mother. She comes in many forms. She is breathing, but she is dying. She may look young, but inside she has become ancient. She smiles, but her heart sobs. She walks, she talks, she cooks, she cleans, she works, she is, but she is not, all at once. She is here, but part of her is elsewhere for eternity."
>
> - Author unknown

Megan, a 36-year-old PR manager, lost her 8-month-old daughter Mary three years ago. When she walked in for her session, I wondered what brought this radiant, strong, cheerful woman into therapy. No one would ever read any signs of sadness or grief in her. She sat in the chair, adjusted her blue silky blouse, rearranged her curly hair, asked for a glass of water, and started telling her story.

Megan met her husband through work. Greg was smart, fun, eloquent, charming, and they seemed to have a strong chemistry. Their whirlwind romance swept Megan off her feet. Six months after they met, their families and numerous friends were celebrating their wedding. Megan found out she was pregnant during their honeymoon in the Caribbean. Back home, the search for a new house started. It was not too long before Megan and Greg moved into the new house and occupied themselves with decorating the baby room and making plans for their future.

The arrival of their daughter Mary was a happy moment. Megan felt loved and cherished, and her Greg was besotted with the baby and surrounded both Megan and the baby with all the love and care possible. Megan enjoyed her maternity leave, but she could not even imagine trusting her little one to a nanny and tried to delay going back to work for as long as she could. When Mary was four months old, Megan gathered her courage and asked her boss to allow her to work part-time. She didn't want to be away from her daughter for more than 4-5 hours a day, and offered to work additional hours from home. Fortunately, Megan's boss accepted.

Greg and Megan enjoyed every minute of their daughter's development. She was a perfect baby: calm, cheerful, and always smiling. Megan found many friends with babies of the same age and they would go for walks together, arranging to meet at each other's houses where their kids would crawl around and laugh together.

Then came a terrible flu. Mary got a fever. At first Megan didn't think it could be serious: she gave her some Panadol and called the doctor, who advised her to watch for any other symptoms and to bring Mary in if she got worse. No new symptoms appeared, but the fever came and went. Mary looked pale and weak, wasn't eating, and wasn't crying much.

Megan called the doctor again on the fourth day. Greg drove them to the doctor's office. Once the doctor saw Mary, Megan knew something was terribly wrong. The doctor called an ambulance and put an oxygen mask on Mary's little mouth straight away. He said he suspected the baby had pneumonia and needed to be admitted to the hospital for treatment. Megan felt the ground slipping from under her feet. Greg looked pale and lost. The ambulance arrived quickly and the emergency team put a drip into Mary's arm vein and carried her out of the doctor's office. Megan was allowed to ride in the ambulance with Mary while Greg followed in the car.

Endless days on the emergency ward began. Mary's condition seemed to stabilize on the first day, but got dramatically worse on the second day. The doctor explained that the tests revealed that atypical pneumonia was at play and that they were trying a combination of antibiotics to treat this difficult bacterial infection. Greg and Megan spent hours and hours in front of Mary's baby cot, watching her little body, plugged into all of the tubes and wires, fighting to take every breath. She was hardly ever awake. Megan stopped eating and she couldn't sleep: her world was now concentrated on this little hospital cot. She remembered the prayers she learned with her grandmother when she was a little girl. Church and religion had never been present in her life after her grandmother passed away; but now Megan was saying all the prayers she could remember.

But no prayers and no doctors' efforts helped. Mary died five days later: her little lungs just gave up. Megan stood in front of the cot, sobbing. Greg was there too: he looked twenty years older, his hands shook, and tears silently rolled down his face.

The hospital brought in some special personnel to help them. Megan says she remembers that different people were trying to talk to them, but she cannot remember what any of them were saying. Some family members organized the funeral, someone took care of the cemetery arrangements, and someone chose the outfit that Mary would wear. Megan collapsed at the grave of her daughter: she simply could not take living and breathing while her little angel was laid to rest in the cold dirty soil.

Megan remembers waking up at home later, after the funeral. Everyone was gone. She wandered around the house and found Greg in the baby room sitting next to the cot, staring at the wall. He couldn't speak. Megan understood he wanted to be alone and sat quietly on the couch in the living room. Night fell, but Greg didn't move.

Megan couldn't stop crying: her pain was ripping out her heart and crushing her head, and there was no escape. The next morning Greg still refused to come out of Mary's room: he sat next to the cot or laid down on the floor. The phone rang nonstop, but neither Megan nor Greg could answer it. Two days passed. Megan felt she was nearing the edge of her sanity. She could not tell what day of the week it was. Greg shut down completely. He was crushed by this loss. Megan began to worry about him. She feared that in this condition, he could harm himself, commit suicide, or have a heart attack. She could not lose him too.

Megan tried to talk to him, then called his parents and sister to come over. Nobody could get through the wall of his silence. The only thing Greg would mutter was "Leave me alone." Megan needed Greg's support; she wanted to share her pain with him, and his withdrawal caused her even more pain.

Megan understood that she could not sit on the couch at home anymore. Everything in the house reminded her of Mary. The loss was unbearable. One week after the funeral, Megan picked up the phone and called her boss. "I need to come back to work," she said. "Full-time," she added.

The next day Megan got up at 6 a.m., and by 7 she was out of the house. She went to the church and prayed in front of the icons for two hours, then went to the office and returned home late. Greg was sleeping on the couch, still wearing the same clothes he had worn at the funeral. He hadn't taken a shower since, didn't shave, and would hardly eat. Megan covered him with a blanket. Greg opened his eyes, looked at her in resentment, didn't say a word, turned around, and slept again.

Megan was out of the house by 7 a.m. the next morning again. She felt that work was providing a necessary distraction: she could think of something other than her loss, and could pretend that her daughter had never died. People in the office asked how she was doing, but Megan brushed away any discussions. "I am ok, thank you," was all she would say.

There was a late meeting in the office on Megan's second day at work. She didn't have to stay, but she couldn't bear the thought of going home to the silence and the emptiness of the house, which had become a graveyard where Megan and Greg's life was buried, together with their daughter. Megan returned home around 9 p.m. Greg was gone. He had left no note. Megan called his parents who said he was at their house and, no, he didn't want to talk to her.

Megan was crushed. She was shaking, and hysterical sobs took over her body. She fell asleep on the couch where Greg had slept the night before. The blanket still smelled of him. In the morning Megan was at church again at 7 and in the office by 9. This would become a daily routine. Megan found peace in the church and distraction in the office. At church, a priest once asked her what brought her there every day, so early. She said she had recently lost her daughter and she believed she could talk to her daughter's soul at church. The priest said: "God sends us only what we can handle, my child; keep praying". So Megan kept praying.

At work she took on more and more new projects, striving to keep herself busy. It felt like meeting deadlines and working late pushed away the time when Megan would come home and have to deal with her pain. She asked her friends and family to clear out Mary's room. Megan felt she would not be able to touch any of her baby's clothes or toys. Megan's friends tried to talk to her about her feelings, but gave up, constantly hearing "I'm ok". They then tried to find a counselor to talk to her. Megan postponed the meeting several times, but when they finally met, she told the counselor that she saw no point of talking about her grief and pain to anyone. "It feels better just to shut out all memories; then the pain can't enter through the closed doors." The counselor suggested that this strategy was counterproductive, but Megan had to take her own time, and so he said he would be ready to help when Megan was ready.

Megan continued living in her routine: church, work, home. It hurt that Greg was not there. He never called and never answered her calls. He sent his sister to collect his clothes. From her, Megan found out that Greg was doing much better: he had returned to work and was seeing a therapist about his grief and depression.

The first Christmas was approaching. Mary would have enjoyed it so much... but Megan couldn't stand the idea of spending Christmas at her parents' house, where her brother and sisters' kids would be running around and opening presents under the Christmas tree.

Megan called the travel agency and booked herself a trip to Palm Beach, where she sat for hours and hours alone on the beach, watching the ocean and listening to the waves crash. Every sunset, she would order a glass of wine and walk down to the beach. She felt that her life was just like the sun: tired of shining, drowsy, and going down. That Christmas alone on the beach was the first time that Megan realized she must find the strength to face her grief head on. "Not yet, just not yet," she told herself.

In the three years since her daughter died, Megan's life was fully devoted to work and church. Every holiday season, she would run away and fly to some faraway place with a beach. She felt she had to avoid festivities so as to not spoil the mood of her friends and relatives and also not to have to look at everyone's happiness.

At work she wore a bright smile and was cheerful, but never let anyone talk to her about her loss or divorce. Recently she met someone with whom she felt she could fall in love. However, she understood that she needed to deal with her grief before she could open up to that man. She did not want to have things she could not share with him, so she sought me out to help her resolve that.

Megan became a regular client. She was a smart woman and was catching on, very quickly, to all the concepts of bereavement and grief that I had to share with her. Obviously, many years of unprocessed grief had created a lot of blocks. We agreed to go back in time and go through all of the emotions of that time again.

Starting with the visit to Mary's doctor's office, we have analyzed every emotion and every thought that Megan had, to identify those counterproductive blocks and biases. There was guilt for not having protected Mary, of failing as a mother, and there was blame for not having taken Mary to the doctor earlier. "If only I had taken her to the doctor earlier - as soon as she developed fever or the next day - and hadn't waited for four days..." said Megan, "she might still be alive".

There was sadness over losing Greg. "He left me because I didn't know how to help him in his grief," said Megan. "The truth is, I didn't know how to deal with it myself, or how to survive this loss. How could he expect me to take care of him at that moment?"

Self-blame and overwhelming guilt are characteristics of parental grief. Parents feel responsible for safeguarding their child's well-being, and their failure to do so becomes engraved in their minds as guilt. Events and situations beyond parental control and protection are hard to accept in these situations.

However, as therapy progressed, Megan learned to deal with the possibility that her daughter's illness was beyond her control. We just couldn't safely assume a change of outcome had she taken Mary to the doctor earlier. The death of the child could have come from the wrong choice of antibiotics, and that would have happened even if the treatment had been initiated days earlier. Overall, there is no possible way to know what could and could not have happened. The events that happened cannot be reversed or undone, and have to be accepted. And the events that had happened had occurred through no fault of Megan. Megan was grateful to accept a "non-guilty verdict".

She blamed herself for not being kind enough to her husband at the time of loss, which the two of them have dealt with so differently. Extensive discussions of the nature of grief and of the fact that grief affects people differently helped her realize that there are no rules to grief, and that as much as she blamed herself for not being kind, her husband was probably going through the same self-blame crusade.

After some months of therapy, Megan felt empowered to reach out to Greg to tell him how sorry she was for the breakup in their relationship. It was helpful for Megan to hear that Greg regretted not doing enough to support Megan and didn't blame her for what had happened.

The last I heard from Megan, she and Greg were meeting regularly to visit their daughter's grave. Perhaps life would give them another chance.

Helen - Time Stopped

"Grief is itself a medicine".
- William Cowper (1731-1800)

Helen, a 56-year-old accountant, lost her husband Tom and 11-year-old son Jason ten years ago. They died in a car crash together. Helen saw me as a part of her psychosocial rehabilitation after being diagnosed with cancer and while receiving chemotherapy. We talked about her illness, the treatment, and what the diagnosis of cancer meant to Helen, when she suddenly revealed:

"Ever since my husband and my son died, I prayed to God to take my life as well. But I am afraid to die in pain, or to suffer and deteriorate if my cancer treatment is not successful. I want to die like my husband and son: instantly, without knowing what is happening".

"Every time I close my eyes, I feel the strong impact of the car that killed my husband and my son. I feel like I am in the same car with them, and that's how I want to die."

"Would you like to talk about that accident? I think there is a lot of information hidden in your story and experience of that tragic loss." I knew that the dramatic loss of Helen's husband and son would explain her current illness representations and death attitudes. Mostly, illness beliefs are formed by experiences and information the patient has received before becoming ill or during the onset of the illness.

During the course of illness, the beliefs may change depending on the patient's establishment of a trustful relationship with the medical practitioner and her participation in available patient education programs or recommended self-education. Illness beliefs influence the patient's coping style.

"I could talk about that non-stop. The truth is that it has been 10 years, people around me have moved on, and I can't talk about that loss to anyone, anymore. My life stopped on that sunny warm day when my husband picked up our son from his tennis club and they drove home for dinner. Dinner was long ready, and I was waiting for them and watching my favorite talk show. They were supposed to be home already, but were running late, I thought. I tried calling, but my husband's mobile was switched off. Then I remember that the phone rang. I answered it and the male voice on the line told me there had been an accident and that he was sorry, but both my husband and my son had died. These words still ring in my head. Life before that moment passed in front of my eyes like a fast-forwarded movie: my husband, our life together, my beautiful boy, his first steps, words, hugs, and all the happiness in our home - it all stopped at once, with one phone call."

"Time stopped, and it never moved again. I never lived again, have never been happy again."

Helen kept quiet for a while. We both sat in silence. I felt that she needed to take a break before we could start talking again.

"I often wondered, why me, why us? What did I do wrong? Why was God so cruel to take my husband and my son and to leave me alive? I have been more dead than alive all of these years."

"Every night I stayed awake, unable to sleep, missing Tom and Jason and crying my eyes out."

"They told me their deaths were sudden and instant. The drunk driver behind the wheel of the other car didn't notice the red traffic light and crushed into my husband's car at full speed, smashing it and killing them both instantly. I only pray and hope that this was indeed the case and that they didn't suffer, didn't understand what happened to them, and that they were not afraid to die. I wish I was there with them."

Helen's wish to have been in the same car with her family very much influenced her expectation of death as a sudden and unconscious event. As we tried to talk about the different types of death and discuss different philosophical approaches to the subject of death, Helen mentioned that after having been diagnosed with her cancer, she started fearing death and dying.

As much as she wanted to join her husband and her son in their afterlife, she was afraid of the pain and suffering associated with death from cancer.

"Helen, what is your life like today? How do you cope with your grief?"

"I found the strength to volunteer in the local community. We established a charity to fight drunk driving by producing educational materials about the effects of this dangerous behavior. We organize a yearly charity event, and the proceeds help us publish enough materials to distribute at local schools, colleges and bars. I find that doing something to prevent accidents like the one that took the lives of my husband and my son gives me a sense of purpose: a feeling that I am doing something for my husband and son, for their memory. I would do anything to keep them alive. And when I am working for this good cause, I feel they are alive next to me."

"But I am also afraid of dying, now. I can't die. I have to live to keep their memory alive."

Helen fought her cancer bravely. It was a hard battle, with several courses of chemotherapy and radiotherapy bringing the loss of hair, energy, and vitality.

I saw her again two years later. She was still afraid of the cancer returning, and of not being able to fight it again. But she said time had started moving again. She was noticing winter days and then spring blossoms, summer joys, and autumn leaves. There was a movement of time, a change of seasons, and a hope for the future. And that was life.

Loss of a Sibling

"I was scared of living a life not worth the living. Why did I deserve to live when my sister had died? I was responsible now for two lives, my sister's and my own, and, damn, I'd better live well."
— Nina Sankovitch, *Tolstoy and the Purple Chair: My Year of Magical Reading*

The relationship between siblings is the longest significant relationship of a lifetime. Siblings are an integral part of each other's life from birth: they share genetic blueprints, family traditions and history, understand the family dynamics, and maintain a bond throughout their lifetimes. An even stronger bond is maintained between twins who share developmental milestones, complimenting each other and forming each other's identity and outlook on life. An elder sibling often serves as an example for the younger one, being idealized and followed in appearance, behavior, hobbies, and interests, while the younger sibling becomes a patronized one for the elder, who feels a responsibility to protect them which is often encouraged by parents and usually carried on through life.

Siblings who preserve a close relationship into adulthood are a part of each other's life events - birthdays, weddings, divorces, child upbringing, and career developments. They may confide in each other more than in any other person in their life and understand that through the bond with their sibling, which is the longest lasting in their life, they not only share the past and the future, but are likely to still be a part of each other's lives as they age. The loss of a sibling, therefore brings devastation and despair and shock and disbelief as the relationship, which was supposed to last till later in life, breaks up abruptly.

Siblings count on each other's support during the eventual loss of their parents and usually share the burdens of funeral arrangements, inherit the property, and help with dissolving their deceased parents' household. The death of a sibling also awakens own mortality fears and sparks recognition of the temporary nature of life.

Despite the closeness of the sibling relationship in life, the grief of a sibling is often overlooked as parents, spouses and children take the central place. Sibling grief can even be included in a form of disenfranchised grief, which is the grief that is neither publicly recognized nor afforded the right of extended mourning. Siblings remain with their grief and go through a longer period of grieving as they say goodbye not only to the past - their childhood and adolescence memories - but also to the future. Siblings do not expect to lose each other early and feel guilty for surviving their sibling, for not having done enough to help or prevent the death, for having disagreements with their sibling, or for not expressing how they value their relationship and the important role the sibling played in their life.

Philip - A Fairytale Sister

"There is sacredness in tears. They are not the
mark of weakness, but of power. They speak
more eloquently than ten thousand tongues.
They are the messengers of overwhelming
grief… and unspeakable love."
— Washington Irving (1783-1859)

Philip, a 45-year-old real estate investor, was referred to me by his treating physician with debilitating symptoms of severe hyperchondriasis and anxiety, often culminating in panic attacks. In his first two sessions I collected his personal history and the nature of his complaints, and we talked about his parents and education. Philip described his anxiety as intense episodes of weakness and dizziness that overwhelm him. During such moments he feels that he is about to die, and he panics.

Fear of death became a prominent topic in our sessions. When we discussed his first encounters with death, he revealed he was born five years after his elder sister died. The loss of his sister must have been unbearable to Philip's parents: they talked about her often. Diane was a wonderful girl: kind, smart, and bright at school. She died at the age of 10 due to complications of a postponed appendicitis surgery.

Philip family's grief was beyond comprehension. Philip's grandmother didn't survive the loss of her granddaughter and died of a heart attack several days after Diane's funeral. Philip's parents tried to keep strong for each other, but even when Philip was born five years later, Philip's mother still visited the cemetery and stayed at Diane's grave every day. Philip remembers playing at her grave, and her picture on the stone monument.

Obviously, Philip's parents turned out to be overprotective of their son. His life was not to be risked. Philip's mother would become paranoid at the sign of any illness, demanding that several doctors to examine him to exclude any possibility of a complication. When Philip joined a basketball club at school, his mother insisted on attending every training and game to make sure Philip would get her first aid in case of any injury. During one of the games, Philip got hit by the ball. It turned out to be a serious eye injury, and short of losing the eye, Philip was not to ever train again.

Throughout his elder years, Philip parent's attention to his health and well-being prevailed but gave way to their own failing, frail health. Within a year of one another, Philip's mother and father passed away. Philip married his high school sweetheart and they had two kids, one after another. Philip's work in real estate, first as an agent and then as an investor, turned out to be very successful in the booming economy of the times. Years of happiness and busy work life followed.

At some point, Philip decided to retire and move to a sunny Mediterranean country. After settling in on a stunning villa on the sea front, Philip's first episodes of weakness and anxiety occurred. During those episodes, Philip felt he was unable to walk, work, or do anything. He felt he was about to die, and extreme fears of dying conquered his mind.

After numerous visits to the ER and extensive check-ups, Philip's doctors all agreed that there was no condition requiring attention. Philip's blood work came back normal except for a minor cholesterol level elevation that was addressed with a drug prescription. Philip was advised to watch his diet, relax, and seek psychological help if his symptoms persisted.

This is when Steven entered my office. He was worried about his health, about his daily conditions of weakness and anxiety, and about not being able to function as he used to.

"What are your memories of your parents and their attitude towards your sister's death?" I asked Steven when he recalled his first encounter with death.

"I remember them talking about her ever since I can remember myself. It was not just my parents, but all other relatives as well. They told me she was a wonderful girl and that it was a tragedy that her life was cut so short."

"Growing up, do you remember feeling worried about your life or your health? Were you worried that something would happen to you like it did to your sister?"

"I do remember it, now. I haven't actually thought about that for many years. I remember that, especially when I was at the age when she died (around ten or eleven years old), I felt very scared. I could hardly fall asleep at night. I constantly felt "imaginary" pains in my belly and was afraid to tell anyone about them. But since nothing bad happened, I gradually calmed down and forgot about it. I started playing basketball, and that brought a lot of joy into my life. After the eye injury, I so much wanted to recover and go back to my team and our trainings (something that was never going to happen) that I never thought a serious condition could threatening my life or health. But now… I feel like I have a fear similar to that I had when I was a child or that something irreversibly bad could happen to me."

"What would the 'irreversible' be?"

"Death. I fear dying like Diane did, when her appendicitis burst because it was diagnosed too late. I feel that even after all of the check-ups and doctor's exams, there still may be something they haven't looked for; something undiagnosed."

"Philip, the fear of death is a universal, most common fear that every human being lives with. At times this fear becomes more acute and at times it subsides. However, there is one important message that the fear of death brings us. Fear of death serves as an "awakening experience". In other words it teaches us to live our life to the fullest extent and to enjoy every day and every interaction we have, encouraging us to make radical changes to our lives. The thought of death gives us renewed energy to live, to make major changes, to be happy, to do what we think is important (i.e. show our loved ones how much we care, ask for forgiveness, forgive others and ourselves, or let go). The idea of death is a catalyst of change, improvement, and forgiveness."

"Often, we see that fear of death is a message our internal voice sends us when we postpone doing something important. This may involve postponing an overdue forgiveness, or postponing putting affairs in order. Many people dealing with acute death anxiety find out that when they have sorted out all financial and emotional pending affairs - everything they would like to have sorted out before they die - the fear of death suddenly subsides. So, in a way, fear of death is actually the fear of not completing important tasks before dying. For example, can we talk about the tasks which would be important to you if you were diagnosed with a terminal illness and knew you only had 3 to 6 months of life left?"

Philip's worldview truly changed after that session. He reevaluated his life goals and priorities, embraced major changes, and revisited to decisions he had been postponing for a long time. We continued working in therapy for another 2 months and consistently noted a decrease in anxiety and hypochondriasis. Philip experienced an emotional turnaround, leading him to feel in control of his state of health and his life.

Grief always brings with it the realization of our own mortality, awakening inherent death anxieties and serving as a confirmation of the finiteness of life. Although at frst we may consider this fear and anxiety as negative and disturbing feelings, there is a strong and positive lesson that the fear of death brings us. It's the lesson that life gives us numerous possibilities and the ability to take action, to make decisions, to make changes, and to say "I love you", "Forgive me", and "I forgive you". Martin Heidegger, a prominent German philosopher, defined death as "the impossibility of further possibility". And so, the fear of death reminds us that we still have the time and ability to do all that we think is important to us.

Peter - One Son Too Many

"When we walk to the edge of all the light we have and take the step into the darkness of the unknown, we must believe that one of two things will happen. There will be something to stand on or we will be taught to fly."
— Patrick Overton, *The Leaning Tree*

Peter, a 52-year-old financial adviser, lost his 31-year-old brother Michael ten years ago. Michael died of a heroin overdose. He had been an addict for a long time. Michael's death still haunted Peter many years later, although his initial reason to seek therapy was for depression. Peter felt the world didn't recognize his abilities or appreciate his efforts. He felt he made a lot of sacrifices for those around him, showering them with love and kindness. His personal life was a collection of similar scenarios of falling in love with a woman, idealizing and worshipping her, giving her everything he could, and then discovering she didn't appreciate all that he did. Eventually there was a breakup, as Peter could no longer take feeling underappreciated.

When we started working on Peter's depression, I suggested looking at why other people's opinions and evaluations of his actions mattered so much to Peter.

"All of my life I sought approval from those around me. I did all I could, but was still not good enough for them." Peter then opened up and told me the story of his relationship with his parents and the loss of his younger brother.

Michael was a late child for Peter's and Michael parents, who was very much loved and spoiled by their undivided love for their little boy. Peter often felt deprived of his parents' attention and jealous of his little brother until later, when he learned to accept Michael's priority in the eyes of their parents.

"How did that make you feel, Peter?"

"As a child, I remember protesting and trying everything I could to get their attention. I fought with other boys in the street, broke windows in the nearby shops, and made trouble at school. Until the age of 15, I was impossible to deal with. But the more I did that, the more I felt my parents were distancing themselves from me and recognizing that Michael was an angel and I was their ongoing trouble."

"I gave up… and convinced myself I was not good enough for my parents, and not worthy of their love. Three years later I finished school and enrolled in military service. I was posted abroad for two years with rare exchanges of letters with my parents. When I got back, my brother Michael was 9. He was close to the age I was when he was born. I watched, with pain, how my mother hugged and kissed him all the time and how my dad arranged his schedule to free up his time to take Michael to swim and play tennis in the afternoons. Nobody ever did that for me."

"I could not live at home any longer. I temporarily stayed with a friend from the army until I found a job unloading cargo at the train station and was able to rent a room in the suburbs of town. Those were hard times. I worked for 10-12 hours a day to make ends meet. I knew my family was somewhere close by, but they didn't seem to care if I had a plate of food in front of me at night…"

"A year later, another army friend was starting his own business and asked if I wanted to join him. It was a popular (back then) model of foreign currency exchange outlets. We rented one small shop initially and started buying and selling currencies. We worked 24 hours a day: first by ourselves, then we were able to hire employees, then we opened twelve more locations around town. Business was doing good."

"During that time, my family contacts were limited. I was invited to family dinners at Christmas and to Michael's birthdays. My parents asked if I had decided to get a degree yet. Every time I would say I had no time for that, they would tell me I was wasting my life and they would wrap up the discussion. They were not interested in the business I was doing, what I was earning, or how and where I lived. Because I didn't have a degree, they labeled me a failure."

"Michael was growing up. I tried to arrange times to catch up with my little brother, to take him to the movies, or have lunch together. He was a good boy and we had a good relationship, open and trusting. He knew I was not happy with how our parents treated me, he felt divided between his love for his parents and his desire for me, as his brother, to spend more time with them. I tried to convince him there was nothing that could be done. Our parents lived by their own rules."

"In the meantime, Michael finished school. He had excellent grades, got offers from several good universities, and started studying towards becoming a lawyer, just like our father."

While at law school, Michael was a popular chap. Dad never limited his pocket money. He felt proud of his student son. The dream of a son following in his footsteps was coming true and gave him enormous pleasure. The problems started with the parties that Michael was famous for organizing. Alcohol fbwed freely, people coveted an invitation, and eventually drugs made their appearance. Michael started using cocaine. He even told his brother that it helped him with his exams - his brain worked in "super-mode", and he finished law school "on a high".

Dad arranged for Michael to work in his law firm. Everyone said he had a bright future. But the cocaine use turned into addiction, and the addiction soon demanded a stronger drug.

Heroin entered the picture. Peter's business by then had expanded to investments, and he branched out into financial advising. Life was busy and money was good. One morning Peter's phone rang. It was his father. He said that Michael had been found dead at his apartment. Police were called and were investigating. It looked like a heroin overdose. Peter's father asked Peter to come and be there while he broke the news to their mother.

Peter still vividly remembers his mother's screams and sobs. She was crushed by the news. Her beloved son was a drug addict … no way; that could not have been true. Michael was dead - no, no, no…

Peter's father was devastated, as well. All of his life had been devoted to the boy. How could he miss drugs? How could he have not noticed that Michael was having a problem???

"After the funeral, I looked at my parents. They had aged 30 years in just a couple of days. Their life was finished, with the death of Michael. My mother didn't want to leave the cemetery; she wanted to be close to her son. Dad suffered a stroke a couple of days later, and he was paralyzed. I was in and out of the hospital taking care of his treatments, rehabilitation, and recovery and making endless trips to doctors and physiotherapists, while driving my mother daily to the church and the cemetery. My life turned into one of a full-time caregiver for my parents. My business was in the hands of my partner, who understood that I needed some time off."

"My parents never thanked me for what I was doing for them. They took it for granted. Their best son was gone and nothing else mattered. Just like when I was a child, the feelings of worthlessness and neglect came back. I felt bitter, depressed, and unable to find love and appreciation from the people closest to me. I loved my brother, but at the same I hated that he took all of my parents' love and pushed me out of the family."

Peter's feelings of low self-worth and under-appreciation were characteristic of depression. Depression drains energy and motivation, encouraging a negative way of thinking. A depressed person will always look at the situation from a pessimistic point of view and promptly deem it hopeless. Depression also makes it difficult for a person to connect on a deep emotional level with anyone, or to accept that other people will love and care for him or her. Peter's depression didn't allow him to see that he was all that his parents had left in their lives.

During the course of therapy, Peter learned that the weight of his hurt and pain always stood in the way of his living a happier life. His forgiveness of his parents' love towards his younger brother allowed him to get rid of a huge burden. Every depression, when thoroughly analyzed, will reveal an experience of being offended by someone, with the pain of it being continuously carried by the depressed person. "He hurt me", "he left me", "they didn't love me enough", "she robbed me of my happiness" - these are the phrases you will come across during a therapy with a depressed person. The automatic reaction to these beliefs is to start behaving as an offended child, acting pitiful, isolating yourself from those "who offended or didn't appreciate you enough", or being sad and miserable ("go lie down and cover your head with a blanket"), waiting for the offender to come and apologize profusely or for parents to make all the troubles go away.

And if that doesn't happen, the depressed person strengthens his or her belief of not being worthy of apology or sufficient love. The way out is to take responsibility for the events in one's life, understanding that you are only hurt when you allow that to happen, that people won't leave you and don't have a responsibility for your happiness to begin with, and that only you yourself are responsible for being happy, and nobody's presence in your life can determine that.

Peter's road to emotional recovery was long and bumpy. He had to accept the painful realization that he had been hurt by his own expectations and not his parents' actions. He had to accept that of the two of them (Peter and Michael), Peter was the strongest in dealing with life and surviving its hardships while Michael was weakened by the "ease of life" and seduced by an abundance of drugs and money.

Peter acknowledged that his protests and outbursts as a child didn't make it easy for his parents to embrace him, and that the arrival of Michael into the family required his mother to concentrate more on the younger child. Peter also realized he still loved his parents and could not judge them for any of their actions, as love between parents and children is unconditional and can't be regulated by blame, false expectations, or pretenses.

Loss through Suicide

You can shed tears that she is gone,
or you can smile because she has lived.
You can close your eyes and pray that she'll
come back,
or you can open your eyes and see all she's
left.
Your heart can be empty because you can't
see her,
or you can be full of the love you shared.
You can turn your back on tomorrow and live
yesterday,
or you can be happy for tomorrow because of
yesterday.
You can remember her only that she is gone,
or you can cherish her memory and let it live
on.
You can cry and close your mind,
be empty and turn your back.
Or you can do what she'd want:
smile, open your eyes, love and go on.
- David Harkins (1960 - present)

The death of a loved one always brings intense suffering, despair, helplessness, hopelessness, anger, anxiety, and depression. In cases of death through suicide, these feelings are even stronger because it is an unexpected loss, with presumed emotional suffering of the deceased leading to the decision to voluntarily take one's life.

The grievers replay the feelings of rejection and isolation their loved one must have experienced before making the decision to die. To make matters worse, suicide carries a stigma, is condemned by society and religion, and is labeled as a loss unworthy of grieving and mourning. Many relatives of suicide victims react to a suicide with silence, secrecy, and denial that death was a suicide. Some religions do not accept honoring the memory of a suicide victim with a church service or allow burial of the deceased within the church cemetery.

Society's negative reactions toward both the deceased and his family make the grief after a loss of a loved one by suicide even more difficult. The inability to mourn openly or in public and the perception of society's judgment for not having prevented the suicide all weigh heavily on grievers. Suicide survivors often report a wall of silence that goes up around them. People prefer not to talk to them about suicide, and distance themselves to avoid interaction.

Families of the suicide victim, especially siblings or children of a parent who committed suicide, are further stigmatized, since society attributes suicide to hereditary factors. Grief is further aggravated by the involvement of police and the possible intrusion of the press. All of these factors allow us to add grief over a suicide victim to the category of disenfranchised grief.

There are some differences in grief over a suicide victim by kinship; for example, the loss through suicide of a spouse, sibling, child, or parent. When parents lose their child through suicide, it is a sudden and very traumatic loss. They can't find any explanation and questions keep spinning in their minds that can never be answered. Pain, anger, and deep sorrow add to the guilt of not having protected their child.

Social support is scarcely available, as there are not many who are brave enough to address the grief of the parents and their emotions. When a spouse commits suicide, the remaining spouse has to deal with feelings of betrayal and the realization that the spousal union that was supposed to have shared trust has failed.

All losses due to a suicide share a greater risk of a complicated grief, less emotional support, and greater depression. Suicide survivors may go through longer periods of denial, confusion, reality distortion, guilt, self-blame, anger, frustration, feelings of worthlessness, or hopelessness and helplessness. There is a very strong belief among the relatives of a suicide victim that they played some role in causing the suicide, or that they could have said or done something to prevent it.

Suicide survivors torture themselves by replaying last communications, trying to remember every small detail that could answer the question "why".

The major feelings from surviving grief after suicide are depression, anger, guilt, and shame.

Depression is the most common symptom in any grief. It is the stage that comes after denial, bargaining and anger. However, in grief after suicide, depression is highly likely to become pathological. The survivor of the suicide sinks further into despair, apathy, and emptiness, is not able to function, has trouble concentrating, and develops negative self-perceptions.

There is an important distinction between the sadness of grief and pathological depression. Sadness in grief focuses on the absence of a loved person, while in depression they focus on one's self, and feelings of helplessness or hopelessness about current or future situations.

Guilt and shame often remain unrecognized and are disguised by the survivor as self-blame, embarrassment, and perception of one's own failure. Guilt and shame develop when an individual relates one's own behavior and situation to what is deemed acceptable, virtuous, or moral by society.

Very often shame and guilt are used interchangeably: however, there is an important distinction between the two terms. Shame refers to the perceived defect in a self-image, while guilt lies in the perceived act or behavior and the consequences of such.

Anger in survivors of suicide may be more intense than in other types of losses. Anger towards the deceased is based on feelings of abandonment, rejection, violation of trust, deprivation of a future together, and the loss of dreams and joy. Survivors of suicide may find it difficult to commit to a trusting relationship in the future.

Anger may also be directed at anyone who has failed to prevent the suicide and at a society which condemns suicide and offers less compassion and support than if the death had been a natural one. Suicide survivors may experience anger towards their religion for failing to honor the deceased and for not providing comfort to the relatives and support with burial services as it would have if the death had been a natural one. There may even be anger at God for having let the suicide happen or anger at oneself for not having "sensed" the suicide was going to happen and for not having prevented the suicide, even though all clues were there. This anger turns into guilt and shame and the cycles of these feelings, together with depression, keep on replaying themselves in the minds of suicide survivors.

It is important to recognize when the suicide survivor is sinking deeper into the vicious cycles of shame, guilt, depression, and anger, and to provide help to restore life and move forward.

Steve - A Letter from Virginia Woolf

"I can't go on spoiling your life any longer. I don't think two people could have been happier than we have been."
- Virginia Wolf (1882 - 1941)

Steve, a 56-year-old network engineer, lost his 47-year-old wife Linda six years ago. Linda lived with bipolar disorder all of her life. Bipolar disorder is also called "manic depression". It is a condition that causes extreme shifts of mood. People with a bipolar disorder often describe it as being on a roller coaster. For weeks they may feel like they are on top of the world, and then they plunge into weeks or sometimes even months of relentless depression. The length of each high and low is unpredictable.

When depressed, Linda would be sad, have no energy, be unable to work, and would lose any interest in life. She would spend most of her days in bed asleep or just laying down, and would not take a shower for days or change her clothes. There would be thoughts about suicide.

But during a manic phase, Linda was "flying". She was euphoric, full of energy, full of plans, would talk nonstop, and would either not sleep for days or would sleep for no more than two hours a day. She would get a lot done, both at home (the house was sparkling, there would be seven- course meals cooked and new recipes tried out) and at work (Linda was a journalist: her writing just seemed to fbw and she would hardly have time to write it down).

And then there was sex. Steve said: "I would give anything to keep Linda in this manic phase. She was the sexiest woman on this planet and she was all I ever wanted: the goddess; the most amazing, seductive, insatiable girl."

"Many of our friends never realized Linda was suffering from a bipolar disorder. They never saw her during one of her depressive episodes. And when they did see her, it would be during a period of her mania, when she behaved as the "soul of the party" and was full of charm, energy, dancing vibes, and humor."

Despite taking mood stabilizers as a maintenance treatment, Linda's mood swings would come abruptly. They could happen within minutes and Steve always prayed that it would not happen while they were out of the house. When a depressive episode would set in, Linda's joyfulness would disappear and it would seem to Steve that some other person had taken possession of her body.

In the state of depression, Linda would often complain of not being able to take this much longer. She felt there was a lot of weight on her shoulders, her body felt heavy, and her head was in a "thick fog". She would talk about ending this torture, and of ending her life. Although Linda's psychiatrist insisted she was to be taken seriously, Steve was sure Linda would never take her life. She just loved her life too much.

And then, one day, Steve came home after work. He closed the entrance door, but the house was dark and silent. He called Linda, but there was no reply. Steve thought her depressive episode might have finished and Linda had found the strength to go out and maybe go to shops or see some friends.

But when he walked into the bedroom, he saw Linda in bed. It looked like she was asleep, but she was dead. An empty bottle of sleeping pills was next to her. Steve called the ambulance and the police, and then he saw an envelope on Linda's bed stand which said 'Steve' on it.

In it was a letter: it was signed by Linda's hand, but the signature said 'V'. Later, Steve found out that 'V' stood for Virginia Woolf, a famous English writer and the author of "Mrs. Dalloway" and "To the Lighthouse". She had lived in the first half of the twentieth century and had suffered from bipolar disorder, much like Linda. She had ended her life by committing suicide at the age of 59 and had left a note to her husband. Linda had copied Woolf's note and left it to Steve, as a farewell letter.

"Dearest, I feel certain that I am going mad again. I feel we can't go through another of those terrible times. And I shan't recover this time. I begin to hear voices, and I can't concentrate. So I am doing what seems the best thing to do. You have given me the greatest possible happiness. You have been in every way all that anyone could be. I don't think two people could have been happier till this terrible disease came. I can't fight any longer. I know that I am spoiling your life, that without me you

could work. And you will I know. You see I can't even write this properly. I can't read. What I want to say is I owe all the happiness of my life to you. You have been entirely patient with me and incredibly good. I want to say that—everybody knows it. If anybody could have saved me it would have been you. Everything has gone from me but the certainty of your goodness. I can't go on spoiling your life any longer. I don't think two people could have been happier than we have been. V."

"Why do you think Linda left you a note initially wrote by Virginia Woolf to her husband?"

"She must have been preparing for this. And in the state that she was in, she probably felt incapable of putting her thoughts down or writing anything. She must have come across this note and found everything in it that she wanted to tell me. That's what I want to believe."

"In the days after Linda's death, I felt so guilty for leaving her alone, for not listening to Linda's psychiatrist and not checking her into a hospital when her depressive episode set in. But the truth is, Linda didn't like the psychiatric ward and felt imprisoned there, and I couldn't do that to her."

"I still believe it was my fault that she died."

"Steve, I think you are forgetting that it was Linda's illness, her bipolar disorder, that lead her to commit suicide, not you," I said carefully. Steve nodded, so I continued. "You understand that if she didn't suffer from bipolar disorder and had not been going through those terrible swings of depressive and manic episodes, she would have not contemplated and went through with the suicide."

"It sounds to me like the note she left you says everything so beautifully. She loved you, and she didn't want you to suffer because of her and her illness. She wanted to end her life because she felt she couldn't fight anymore. She thought of you, not herself."

Steve couldn't hold back his tears. He covered his face with his hands and sobbed uncontrollably.

"I can't bear the thought that she went through this alone. I was not there to tell her how much I loved her and how her illness never made my life difficult. I was so grateful for having Linda in my life, and I cherished every minute we had together - good or bad."

"Linda often said her mind and body lived two separate lives." Steve smiled as he said that. "She said, "I get depressed when my mind gets tired of dealing with my weak body and leaves, and then when my body is ready, my mind returns and there is life in my body again."

"Do you think Linda's body got tired of waiting for her mind to return? Do you think this means Linda's mind is not dead, and is out there?" asked Steve.

"Steve, there certainly is a point in what you are asking. During grief, people realize one important thing: the person they loved may have died, but the relationship with that person continues. It may continue through mental communication, through commemorating the deceased, through remembering important dates and places, and even through visiting the cemetery or church to pray for and honor the memory of the deceased loved one."

"Linda's mind, her personality, and her soul will always be with you in your mind, in your memories, and in your life - with you for as long as you choose to keep her alive."

Julie - Why him?

"Mourning is one of the most profound human experiences that it is possible to have… The deep capacity to weep for the loss of a loved one and to continue to treasure the memory of that loss is one of our noblest human traits."
- Edwin Shneidman (1918-2009)

Julie, a young woman in her thirties, came in for a session to figure out a way of dealing with her anxiety. Julie worked as a public relations and marketing consultant, and initially I thought her anxiety was work related. However, the story Julie told me clearly shows how unresolved grief (in this case over a father who committed suicide five years earlier) can bring with it severe dysfunction to surviving relatives.

It was a Christmas day, when Julie was spending with her fiancé's family, that she received a call from her older sister telling her that their father had taken his life. Five years later, Julie could still describe that moment in fine detail, and her pain remained intense. Sobbing, she kept repeating, "How could this have happened to me and my family?", "Why us?", "Why him?"

Julie's parents divorced when she was three years old, and she spent her childhood moving from one home to another. Her older sister was always an example for Julie: she looked up to her and wanted to be like her.

Julie's mother was an energetic and ambitious woman, and the divorce empowered her to succeed in her career and provide the best she could for her daughters. Julie's father was a different personality. Yes, he was hard working and wanted to provide the best for his two daughters, but he was a true hippy at heart. He loved his free time, his meditations, and soul searching wanderings and chose to be a freelancer rather than being tied to a steady office job.

Julie remembers having the best times when she was at her father's house because no schedule was to be observed, Dad was never angry or upset, the house was always full of his friends, and everyone loved him. Dad's positive energy and bubbly personality were an instant attraction to everyone around him.

But as time passed and Julie's father grew older, his life and personality started to change. As he aged, he was more and more drawn to search for his purpose in life. Although he remained the fun-loving man Julie grew up with, his overall character and behavior began to change.

"What do you mean by this, Julie?"

"Looking back, I believe my father started to experience the symptoms of depression. I think it was depression that led him to his actions that Christmas day. I miss my father every day and wish I could just dial the number and hear his voice. So many things have changed since he died, but I still can't find an answer as to why he would do that.

After my father's death, I remember playing the part of a detective with my sister. We searched every inch of his house, sure that we would find something that would help us understand why he had left this world. We went through his books, reading what he had highlighted. We went through his day planner, reading every last note that he wrote to himself.

We searched his emails and went through the history on his computer. We met with his therapist and his friends, and talked to the neighbors. We went through his medicine cabinet, his drawers, and even the pockets of his clothing. I wish I could say that we found something, but we didn't. Still, today, I often catch myself asking WHY..."

"Julie, your questions are very valid. Indeed, overcoming loss is difficult for anyone; however, when the loss is a result of suicide, so many additional thoughts, feelings, and emotions come into play. Many questions come into our minds. "Why did our loved one end his life? What was he thinking or feeling in the moments before he died? Why didn't he reach out for help? Is there anything I could have done to prevent his suicide? How could I not notice that he was thinking of suicide?

"The truth, is you will never know or understand the depth of his pain, or the demons that he faced. These questions will never be answered. And uncertainty is very unsettling. It is human nature to have difficulty accepting what we do not understand. We need answers; we need to understand. And when we can't understand, we become stuck. We continue searching for the answers and this search for meaning after a suicide impacts our ability to grieve and our ability to move forward. Your time and energy is being spent in the past as you try to make sense of the unknown. Spending time trying to figure out "why" and looking for answers only brings more hurt, anger, and guilt.

"However, as time goes by, you will learn that you can find peace in the unknown. Everyone finds their own way. There is no right way to mourn your loss. You do what is best for you in order to become unstuck and move forward. You will still not have the answers to all the WHYs, because the only person who holds the last puzzle piece is your loved one, who is no longer alive. And you have to learn to accept that."

Julie's journey to process her grief was long and complicated. She has gone through painful guilt, through anger outbursts towards her father, blaming him for causing so much pain to her, and through the fear that, when faced with difficulties, she could follow in her father's footsteps.

However, as many other suicide survivors learn, she came to accept the decision of her father as his own and freed herself from the thoughts that she could have done something to prevent the sad outcome of his decision. Holding on to the happy memories and cherishing the lessons her father had taught her in life made Julie understand that he was a unique individual with a vulnerable worldview and fragile self-esteem. Unconditional love for her father was the ultimate medicine that allowed Julie to more forward and incorporate memories of her father in her life.

CHAPTER SEVEN

Grief Outcomes

"Happiness is beneficial for the body, but it is grief that develops the powers of the mind."
– Marcel Proust, *In Search of Lost Time* (1871-1922)

The death of a loved one is one of the most difficult life crises that one can ever face. Coping with such loss often takes a long time, challenging values and beliefs and redefining established roles, relationships, responsibilities, and demands. However, as with any other crisis in life, bereavement can bring personal transformation and personal growth. Personal growth in bereavement may be defined as increased independence, self-reliance, self-efficacy, wisdom, maturity, compassion, and a better understanding of others, as well as changes in life priorities and increased spirituality.

Losing a loved one can be devastating. Every aspect of daily life can seem hard or even impossible to accomplish. The grieving process focuses on major tasks that need to be completed to emerge from grief. These include acceptance of the reality of a changed world, taking time off from the pain of grief, adjusting to a world without the deceased, and developing new connections with the deceased while embarking on a new life. These tasks of grief fulfill the process by allowing a survivor to concentrate on mourning (or adjust to the loss) and improve their functioning to restore their life.

The research on grief and bereavement issues continues to grow as therapists become more aware of the nature and scope of these experiences and the factors that may contribute to the development of pathological grief and the best interventions to choose in treatment. Grief is a process that may take months or even years. Not many people are able to come to terms with their loss at the end of the first year, and some people may require as many as three to four years to achieve emotional stability.

Sharing with the grieving person that something positive will come from their loved one's death is obviously unhelpful, untimely, and unethical. However, research into the experiences of other bereaved individuals may be mentioned as an example. A substantial body of research confirms that significant positive outcomes are associated with bereavement and grief.

The most notable positive outcomes include:

Learning to appreciate the value of life and the need to live in the moment as much as possible

Placing greater importance on spending time with loved ones

Becoming stronger as a result of surviving the pain of death

Becoming more independent by doing things previously done by or together with the deceased

Becoming more mature, self-reliant, and self-confident

Entering into a closer relationship with remaining family members and loved ones

Learning to let loved ones know how much they are loved.

Give yourself enough time and true permission to grieve. Some days will be easier while on other days, you will feel like everything is falling apart. Grief is a roller coaster with unexpected ups and downs, and it is all natural. Tell people around you how you feel and what you need. People may be afraid to contact you or might even avoid you for fear of saying the wrong thing. Reach out to others: it will help you and make them grateful and relieved. In difficult times, think of others who may be going through similarly difficult or perhaps even worse times. Helping them will help you heal yourself.

Think about joining a grief support group: sharing your stories and supporting others will also give you back the love and support of others in the group. It may be helpful to write a journal. Writing down your thoughts and feelings helps "get them out of your system". Do not feel rushed to make any major decisions. Instead, take good care of yourself. You can deal with the necessary changes when you are ready. Get rest when you need it, try to exercise regularly, and eat well. Rest, diet, and exercise are critical to your physical and mental recovery and well-being. And finally, love yourself and believe in yourself. Think of all the qualities your loved one valued in you. You are still the same person: you are unique, strong, loved, and valued - and I wish you the best of strength to find meaning and hope in your future.

CPSIA information can be obtained at www.ICGtesting.com
Printed in the USA
LVOW07s1033270816

502112LV00001B/24/P